Into the Classroom Series

WILLINGLY TO SCHOOL

Religious Education
as an Examination Subject

Patrick M. Devitt

VERITAS

Published 2000 by
Veritas Publications
7/8 Lower Abbey Street
Dublin 1

ISBN 1 85390 581 X

British Library Cataloguing
in Publication Data.
A catalogue record for
this book is available
from the British Library.

Cover design by Bill Bolger
Printed in the Republic of Ireland by Betaprint Ltd, Dublin

CONTENTS

Dedicated to Báirbre, who likes to go to school (most days),
and to Eoin, who tells me that school is often boring.

INTRODUCTION

BACKGROUND TO THE SERIES

Though Religious Instruction has been given in Irish second-level schools for many years, it has not yet been possible to assess this work under the State examination system. The reason for this anomaly is the Intermediate Education Act (1878), which allowed for the teaching, but forbade the State examination, of Religious Instruction. One significant educational event in Ireland recently was the legal battle to repeal the relevant section of this Act, so that Religious Education (RE) could, at last, become a subject for State examination. In anticipation of this legal change, the National Council for Curriculum and Assessment (NCCA) established, in the mid-nineties, a Course Committee on Religious Education. The most recent fruits of its work are the two syllabuses, one for Junior Certificate, published in early 2000, and the other (draft) for Leaving Certificate, published in May 1997. The legal constraint on State examination of RE has since been removed, and ministerial approval has been given for the implementation of these two syllabuses, on a phased basis, beginning with the Junior Certificate syllabus in September 2000.

With the Junior Certificate syllabus due for immediate introduction, and with the prospect of the Leaving Certificate syllabus also in the air, Religion teachers will clearly need some assistance in teaching them. Guidelines[1] for the implementation of the RE syllabuses, in accordance with the ethos of each school, have already been drawn up by the relevant religious authorities. Curriculum changes have also been introduced in the Mater Dei Institute of Education, to take account of these new syllabuses within the pre-career education of many Religion teachers. Already, new textbooks have been written for the Junior Certificate pupils. Many existing teachers will need in-career programmes.

In the context of all these very necessary provisions, two members of the staff of the Mater Dei Institute have co-ordinated the writing,

5

in two phases, of a series of commentaries on the new RE syllabuses. These commentaries have Religion teachers mainly in mind; they aim to help teachers appreciate the riches of the new syllabuses and to grasp the new opportunities provided by them. This is a difficult task, and a daunting challenge; each of the authors realises that not all Religion teachers are happy about the arrival of these new examination syllabuses. However, at a conference in St Patrick's College, Drumcondra, in February 1996, to discuss the place of religion in Irish education, many participants expressed an *optimism* with regard to the advent of Religious Education as an examination subject in the Junior and Senior cycles.[2] An equally optimistic view, based on an experience of Religion teaching in Northern Ireland, was articulated in a recent issue of the magazine *Intercom*.[3] That is the hope-filled spirit in which this series has been written.

Phase One of the series consists of a single volume, entitled *Willingly to School*.[4] This volume is offered to Religion teachers who are about to teach the Junior Certificate syllabus for the first time. It will also prepare them for the eventual challenge of teaching the Leaving Certificate syllabus. It presents a global reflection on the relationship between the two NCCA RE syllabuses and the work of teaching Religion to Catholic pupils in the schools of Ireland today. It asks the following general question, *'How can the NCCA RE syllabuses be integrated into the catechetical work of teaching Religion to Catholic pupils in Irish schools today?'* This is the central question, which determines the shape of the introductory volume.

Phase Two (already in the pipeline) will be introduced later. It will provide a series of thematic commentaries, one for each of the ten sections in the Leaving Certificate RE syllabus. Since members of many different religious persuasions will study this syllabus, the commentaries will be written with this fact clearly in mind.

WILLINGLY TO SCHOOL: AN OUTLINE OF THE ARGUMENT

In *Willingly to School*, I propose to answer the following general question, *'How can the NCCA RE syllabuses be integrated into the catechetical work of teaching Religion to Catholic pupils in Irish schools today?'* It is not by accident that my foundational question mentions Catholic pupils rather than Catholic schools. I assume that Catholic pupils are being offered a catechetical service in a wide range of Irish schools. I hope to show that no matter what school young Irish Catholics attend, their catechetical education today can indeed be enriched by an imaginative presentation of the new NCCA RE syllabuses.

Preliminary Remarks on Catholic Education

The Catholic Church has many different kinds of involvement in education, any one of which could rightly be called 'Catholic education'.[5] The involvement of the Catholic Church in the provision of general educational services to people in need, no matter what religion they belong to, is entitled to be called Catholic education. An example of this would be in New York City, where Catholic Religious orders often run schools in which nearly all the pupils are non-Catholics. Catholic education, in this sense, springs from a Catholic conviction of the value of general education; and is offered to the most needy, by the Catholic Church, in that same spirit of generosity which Jesus preached. A less extreme version of this kind of Catholic education is hinted at in *The Religious Dimension of Education in a Catholic School (RDECS),* which states that not all students of Catholic schools belong to the Catholic Church; in fact, they may not even be Christians (6).[6] *RDECS* does not even assume that all the staff need be Catholics: 'If all share a common faith, this can be an added advantage' (103).[7]

Another very different kind of Catholic education is the general education of people who are Catholics. Here the learners are entirely or nearly exclusively Catholic, and the same is usually true of the staff. In Ireland, the private schools run by clergy and Religious and lay Catholics would clearly fit into this category. So too, of course, would most of the Community Schools and Colleges. Though not managed by Church bodies, these State-sponsored schools provide a rich education for a predominantly Catholic pupil population and are staffed by teachers, many of whom are both Catholic and open to a Catholic philosophy of education.[8] According to one way of describing Catholic schools, these State-sponsored schools might loosely be called Catholic schools: 'What makes the Catholic school distinctive is its attempt to generate a community climate in the school that is permeated by the Gospel spirit of freedom and love'(1).[9] In legal terms, however, these schools are not strictly speaking Catholic because they are not subject to ecclesiastical authority (4).

Yet another kind of Catholic education is the education of people in what it means to be Catholic. In the school context, this is normally called Religious Education *or* the teaching of Religion *or* Religious Instruction, to use the language of *RDECS*. Though this form of religious education might be very discreet in those schools mentioned above, where the majority of pupils are not Catholics, one would expect it to have a pride of place in all Catholic schools, and also in those schools 'that are virtually or *de facto* Catholic'.[10] However, religious education can be downgraded in some Catholic schools because it allegedly takes valuable class-time away from other 'more important' subjects. The argument seems to be: less time for Religion, more time for exam subjects, better results all round.

And yet, the research results of the Australian educationalist Marcellin Flynn are a clear challenge to this argument. His research found that the provision of good religious education did not compromise other school subjects. On the contrary, he found that 'acceptance of the religious message of Catholic schools appears to be associated with achievement in all aspects of life in these schools'.[11] Any attempt at explaining this interesting phenomenon will probably base itself on the well-established notion[12] that Catholic schools accumulate a measure of 'social capital', which generates much of their overall educational success.

Subsidiary Questions to be Examined

School context
In anticipation of a more detailed account of this topic in the Appendix, I should like to mention briefly here the overall *school context* within which the new RE syllabuses will be taught. Catholics believe that the Catholic Church has a mission of evangelisation, and that Catholic schools can make a wide range of contributions to this process of evangelisation. The relevant principles of school

evangelisation, as developed in the Vatican document *RDECS*, are as follows: the integration of faith and culture; school as a privileged place of evangelisation and maturity of faith; the importance of school climate; and, finally, the distinctiveness of catechesis and Religious Instruction. In the Appendix, all of these themes will be explored in more detail, and also related to various aspects of the new NCCA RE syllabuses.

Variety of teaching approaches
It is obvious that Religion teachers have a variety of teaching styles.[13] Since there are so many different catechetical voices, I shall draw upon the work of Robert Newton[14] and try to allow all these voices to speak, especially in Chapter 1 *(What Range of Religion Teachers is One Likely to Find?)* but also in Chapter 2 *(How Do Different Teachers Teach Morality?)*. In this latter chapter, I shall reflect on one of the aims of Section F of the Junior Certificate syllabus, *The Moral Challenge:* 'To show how religious belief is expressed in particular moral visions'.[15] I shall also draw upon the Leaving Certificate Section on *Moral Decision-Making* and show how the 'morality' component of the RE programme can alert catechists to the need for moral dialogue, introduce them to the grammar or structure of moral thinking, and thereby help them in explaining better the moral dimension of faith.

Facets of mature faith
I wish to state clearly at this juncture my own basic educational conviction: helping pupils' faith grow to maturity is the key aim of all catechetical activity in school. This theme of 'maturity of faith' is analysed in the *General Catechetical Directory* (1971).[16] I have already outlined its importance in *That You May Believe* (1992)[17] and further developed the theme in *Immortal Diamond* (1997).[18] There I have suggested that mature faith has many interrelated dimensions or facets: faith as expressed in prayer and ritual can be called its *worship* dimension; faith as understood and explained is its *intellectual* dimension. Faith has a *prophetic* dimension when it colours one's vision of life; faith has an *eschatological* dimension insofar as it helps believers face the future with courage. The *moral* aspect of faith, just mentioned above, provides an inspiring vision and gives shape to one's

values and life decisions. An integral part of mature faith is its *socio-political* dimension, expressed in its slow work for justice and peace. Truly mature faith should be an 'outreach' faith, relating believers to fellow Christians (*ecumenical* dimension) and relating them also to non-Christians (*missionary* aspect).

Fostering faith, directly or indirectly
Before inviting the new NCCA syllabuses to dialogue and debate with my *Immortal Diamond*, I need to mention a critical distinction between strict catechesis and classroom Religion teaching, a distinction that is implicit in *RDECS,* pars. 68-69. According to Crawford and Rossiter,[19] one can help faith to mature either *directly* (through strict catechesis) or *indirectly* (through teaching Religion in class). How faith is fostered *indirectly* in the Religion classroom is the theme of Chapter 3 *(What is the Main Purpose of the Religion Class?).*

The fostering of faith through classroom religious education has to be done in a manner consistent with the ethos of modern-day classrooms, influenced so much by the culture of religious indifference, where God is often 'missing but not missed'.[20] Rather than *directly* pursuing reluctant teenagers with a megaphone, and challenging them bluntly to faith in the Gospel, the Religion teacher needs to help the pupils 'to step back from' faith in order to view it more critically.[21] In this way pupils' faith may indeed be fostered *indirectly;* equally, of course, pupils' faith may not yet bloom within the Religion classroom.

How various aspects of the NCCA syllabuses can indirectly foster faith
With this key point established, I then propose to look in greater detail at the NCCA syllabuses and explain to what extent they might *indirectly* foster the faith of Catholic pupils. I shall emphasise this point most forcefully in Chapter 4, which deals with the *worship* dimension of faith *(How to Teach Prayer?).* The major reference points here will be the Junior Certificate Section E, *The Celebration of Faith,* and the Leaving Certificate Section on *Worship, Prayer and Ritual.*

The Junior Certificate Section B *(Foundations of Religion – Christianity)* aims 'to identify the Gospels as the main source of knowledge about Jesus' (p. 14). And so, the younger pupils will be able to study the Gospels as the foundational texts of Christian faith. Later on, as older adolescents, they will be helped to situate the Gospels in their larger religious and cultural contexts, through a study of the Leaving Certificate Section on *The Bible; Literature and Sacred Text.* Each of these two biblical Sections will provide insight into all the distinct dimensions of mature Christian faith, since the biblical record is the distillation of the living Jewish and Christian faith traditions. However, for the purposes of this book, I shall link the Bible to the *eschatological* dimension of biblical faith. In recognition of the NCCA syllabuses' scriptural perspective, I shall ask the question *'Dare We Hope?'* (Chapter 5), and in my answer I shall present a personal statement of hopeful faith.

The Junior Certificate syllabus 'seeks to promote an understanding and appreciation of why people believe... [it] is built around a framework of knowledge, understanding, skills and attitudes' (p. 4). In a word, it attempts to offer an *intellectual* grounding for religious faith. Two of the proposed Leaving Certificate Sections *(The Search for Meaning and Values* and *Religion and Science)* should also contribute much to the *intellectual* dimension of faith; they should help young people to make more sense of their inherited faith and give them a language in which they can explain that faith to other people. In Chapter 6, I shall focus on the understanding of faith, and ask *'How to give an imaginative account of the faith?'* Given their explicit academic focus, the new NCCA syllabuses ought primarily to enable pupils to achieve an *intellectual* grasp of their mysterious faith, and flowing from that, a ready ability to articulate that faith, systematically and imaginatively.

In Section A, Part 4, of the Junior Certificate syllabus *(Relationships between Communities of Faith),* pupils are introduced to the following key concepts: ecumenism, inter-faith dialogue, sectarianism, religious conflict and tolerance (p. 12). The ecumenical agenda is obvious. Furthermore, the following two Leaving Certificate Sections *(Christianity; Origins and Contemporary Expressions* and *Religion; the Irish Experience)* should also help pupils in their ecumenical outreach. While the challenge of ecumenism is one that concerns all Christians in the present, no ecumenical progress will be possible unless people know how the divisions arose in the past and were consolidated throughout the years. One major reason for teaching Church history today, therefore, is to facilitate ecumenical outreach. This will be the hidden agenda of Chapter 7 (*'Why Teach Church History?'*). However, while recognising how many historically important and ecumenically pertinent ideas can be found throughout the NCCA syllabuses, I shall also recommend that Religion teachers of Catholic pupils would need to complement the very good material in the NCCA syllabuses. Chapters 7 and 10 will each suggest that, from a Catholic point of view, a good grounding in Catholic Church history is needed today and pupils ought to be introduced to a very wide range of people who have successfully lived the Christian gospel in their lives.

The Junior Certificate Section C, entitled *Foundations of Religion – Major World Religions*, is well complemented by the Leaving Certificate Section on *World Religions*. Both sections should assist Religion teachers to explore the missionary dimension of the Christian faith. So I shall ask, *'Why Teach World Religions?'* (Chapter 8). Here I shall listen to both sides of the argument, in favour of *and* against the teaching of world religions.

At Junior Certificate level the issues of justice and peace are introduced, within Section F *(The Moral Challenge)*, and specifically in Part 4, p. 42 *(Religious Morality in Action)*. The Leaving Certificate Section on *Issues of Justice and Peace* will build upon the foundations laid down in earlier schooling. All of this material relates to the *socio-political* dimension of the faith, and so, with an eye upon Catholic Social Teaching, I shall pose the question *'How to Tell Our Best Kept Secret?'* (Chapter 9).

The question I ask in Chapter 10, *'Why Did God Make Us Male and Female?',* is prompted by the sense of prophecy that permeates both Jewish and Christian traditions. It flows, in other words, from the prophetic dimension of both faiths; but it also tries to articulate some prophetic questions for the Catholic Church today. Junior Certificate pupils may indeed have some exposure to the topic of prophecy, but only if they study Section C (*Major World Religions*, p. 22). The same is true at Leaving Certificate level, since everybody may not study the optional Section on *Women, Religion and the Christian Tradition*. This is unfortunate, given the critical role of prophets within various faith traditions.

Conclusion

By asking all of these *subsidiary* questions, in the context of the two new NCCA syllabuses, my original *foundational* question can finally be answered. I maintain that the new NCCA syllabuses in Religious Education ought to provide much valuable assistance to Religion teachers for their catechetical work in Irish second-level schools. Not only that, but the challenging content of these syllabuses should also enrich the more general life of the entire Catholic Church in Ireland. My hope is that, once teachers appreciate this, their classrooms will become 'hospitable spaces for learning'[22] and their teaching will encourage their pupils to creep less 'like snail' and to come more 'willingly to school'.

Notes

1. See Irish Catholic Bishops' Conference, *Guidelines for the Faith Formation and Development of Catholic Students: Junior Certificate Religious Education Syllabus.*

2. For the proceedings of this conference, see P. Hogan and K. Williams (eds.), *The Future of Religion in Irish Education,* and in particular pp. 18, 52, 54, 115 and 123.

3. A. Kinsella, 'Teaching religion as an exam subject', *Intercom* (February 1999), pp. 24-25.

4. With apologies to W. Shakespeare's school children, 'creeping like snail unwillingly to school' (Jaques, *As You Like It,* Act 2, Sc. 7).

5. See P. M. Devitt, *How Adult is Adult Religious Education?,* pp. 139-140. For a brief historical overview of Catholic education, see J. P. Marmion, *Catholic Traditions in Education.*

6. Sacred Congregation for Catholic Education (Rome, 1988). In my text, paragraph numbers are given thus: (6).

7. This openness to a diversity of faith commitments among the staff in a Catholic school is developed even further by D. Sleigh, 'But do they go to Mass? Criterion for Teacher Appointment?' in Australian Province Leaders of the Christian Brothers, *Catholic School Studies* 66, no. 1 (May 1993), pp. 33-34.

8. For an account of the role of vocational schools in Ireland, see D. Murray, *A Special Concern. The Philosophy of Education: A Christian Perspective,* p. 15.

9. Quoting Second Vatican Council, *Gravissimum Educationis,* par. 8.

10. J. M. Feheney, 'The Future of the Catholic School: An Irish Perspective', in J. M. Feheney (ed.), *From Ideal to Action: The Inner Nature of a Catholic School Today,* p. 216.

11. M. Flynn, 'Religious Commitment and School Achievement: Is there a Relationship?' in *Catholic School Studies,* 66, no. 1 (May 1993), p. 24.

12. For a balanced evaluation of the true worth of Catholic schools in America, given by people who are not themselves Catholics, see A. S. Bryk et al., *Catholic Schools and the Common Good;* and J. S. Coleman and T. Hoffer, *Public and Private High Schools: The Impact of Communities.*

13. For an examination of the manner in which one's Christian vision colours the process of teaching, see D. O'Leary, 'The Ministry of Teaching in the Church school', in D. O'Leary (ed.), *Religious Education and Young Adults.* For a good reflection on Jesus the teacher, see K. Treston, *Paths and Stories,* pp. 40-52.

14. R. Newton, 'Four models of teaching religion', in Our Sunday Visitor, *PACE* 11, 1982.

15. Department of Education and Science, *Junior Certificate Religious Education Syllabus,* p. 38.

16. See Sacred Congregation of the Clergy, *Directorium Catechisticum Generale (General Catechetical Directory),* pars. 21-31. A revised Directory was published in October 1997: see *General Directory for Catechesis,* pars. 85-86.

17. See P. M. Devitt, *That You May Believe,* pp. 114-123.

18. See P. M. Devitt, *Immortal Diamond: Facets of Mature Faith.*

19. See M. Crawford and G. Rossiter, *Missionaries to a Teenage Culture,* pp. 65-77.

20. This phrase is much loved and often used by M. P. Gallagher; and is to be found in the work of a Catalan Jesuit, Josep Vives, whom Gallagher quotes in 'The New Agenda of Unbelief and Faith', in D. A. Lane (ed.), *Religion and Culture in Dialogue,* p. 136.

21. J. Fowler notes how adolescents' formal operational thinking enables them 'to reflect on the life course from "above" or "beside" it.' See *Stages of Faith,* p. 71.

22. J. Sullivan, *Catholic Schools in Contention,* p. 185.

Chapter 1

WHAT RANGE OF RELIGION TEACHERS IS ONE LIKELY TO FIND?

No Religion teacher is an island. As well as working within one's own classroom, each Religion teacher is part of a larger school team. If teachers are to work well together, the first thing they need to recognise and accept is that they can differ from one another in many respects. An exploration of such differences will be the focus of this chapter. I shall draw upon a series of articles dealing with the major current approaches to Religion teaching.[1] Anyone who has done the Enneagram knows that there is a wide range of personality types, and so there ought to be many different 'pedagogical orientations'[2] to teaching. An acceptance of one's own personal teaching approach, as well as a valuing of the strengths of other teachers' approaches, are the twin foundations of worthwhile co-operation.

Identifying one's own model
Implicit in everything people do is a set of assumptions about the way things should be done. Everyone works out of some theory or another; teachers are no different. Each teacher has an image of the ideal school, of the perfect teacher, and of the good student. Teachers complain about the curriculum and the evaluation procedures, only because they have a vision (theory) of how these might be improved. When one puts all of these elements together, sometimes they mesh well, like the modern car's gear unit. Occasionally, though, they jar. This is because the teacher is operating partially out of one theory, partially out of another. Perhaps one's idea of the model teacher does not match one's idea of the good student. Or maybe one's idea of the aim of education does not correspond with one's view of the ideal methods of assessment. What teachers need to do is to discover their own model of education. Having discovered it, they need to ask, 'Is it internally consistent?' If it proves not to be so, then it may need to be changed

in some way. If it proves to be consistent, then they still need to ask, 'Is this the one that appears most valid for me now in my teaching?'

Robert Newton faces up to these issues, in the following manner: he outlines four common teaching models – and claims that most teachers operate out of one or other of these. But, because teachers don't always adequately advert to how other people operate out of a different set of assumptions, at times there can be a lack of understanding, and even confusion or conflict, between them. If one were to ask teachers, 'What is the aim of religious education?', there would be different answers; and each would reflect one's own particular assumptions. Each would flow from a particular model. Likewise, if one were to ask about the function of the teacher in religious education, or if one were to try to describe the ideal pupil, the variety of answers would once again reveal the variety of models within which teachers operate.

Newton claims that there are seven elements in the teaching-learning process:
1. Fundamental belief (what Newton calls *First Principle*).
2. *Aim* (or purpose of religious education).
3. Image of the *Teacher*.
4. Role of the *Pupil*.
5. Style of *Curriculum*.
6. *Environment* or *Ethos*.
7. Kinds of *Evaluation*.

Each of Newton's four models gives different answers to these questions. That's why the models are different from one another. They are called **Open Education; Academic; Educational Technology; and Social Reconstruction.**

Foundations and aims

In Open Education, the foundation or *first principle* on which everything else rests is the Augustinian conviction that God is closer to people than they are to their deepest selves. In other words, people are naturally religious; there is a religious dimension to life;[3] God is to be met in a special way *within* one's personal experience. The Anthropological (or Experiential) approach to RE is founded on this assumption. Many aspects of the NCCA syllabuses are also based on this assumption.[4] For example, Junior Certificate Section D (*The Question of Faith*) mentions the young person's 'stages of faith' (p. 29) and relates these stages to the process of 'asking questions, finding answers, [and] imaging God' (JC Section D, 2 and 3).[5] Older adolescents will be introduced to an even richer variety of religious experience in *The Search for Meaning and Values* (LC Section A, 2.2)[6] which explores religious myth, traces of the sacred, religious behaviour and spirituality. The theme of the universal revelation of God, in LC Section A, 3.2, will challenge pupils to explore their experiences reflectively – so that they can actually discover God within these experiences.[7]

Once one accepts this scenario, then the *aim* of religious education is simple – that pupils will develop religiously and become the religious persons they are by nature.[8] Religion is not meant to be pumped into people or added on to them. It is drawn out of them. Education in Religion is a 'leading out' of hidden potential, 'the awakening of something within'.[9] Schools ought not to be like factories, where all pupils are fashioned into identical products. Instead, all pupils should emerge from school with their different talents valued and their diverse potentials developed. At its best, this Open approach to religious education can be an exciting, enriching and challenging process. However, those who object to this Open approach claim that it regularly leads to the abandonment of all genuine religious 'content'.

If, however, a teacher operates out of the Academic model, the *first principle* will be somewhat different.[10] For this teacher, religious development will be of great importance; but the key to this development will be *religious knowledge*. And this knowledge will be available in one's religious tradition long before instruction takes place, and before knowledge arises in the minds of the pupils.[11] Accordingly, the *aim* of religious education will be to confront one's pupils with their religious tradition so that they can come to know and understand it, and be able critically to adapt this tradition to the world of today.[12] Thomas Groome has developed precisely such an educational approach, which aims to insert young people critically into their religious tradition – he calls it 'shared praxis'.[13]

Both NCCA syllabuses provide a rich resource for teachers who use an Academic model. Honours pupils at Junior Certificate level will be 'exploring different views of the relationship between state law and religious morality' (*The Moral Challenge*, JC Section F, 5) or perhaps examining some of the 'new titles for Jesus', such as Son of Man, Son of God, New Creation, and Christ (*Foundations of Religion – Christianity*, JC Section B, 5). All Junior pupils will be expected to become 'familiar with the Christian understanding of sacrament and have a detailed understanding of the place of sacrament in two Christian denominations' (*The Celebration of Faith*, JC Section E, 4).

In the light of growing academic potential among older pupils, LC Section A, 1.2 will examine philosophy as part of the human tradition of searching for meaning; and LC Section A, 3.3b will propose for honours students the traditional proofs for the existence of God. Equally challenging academic material will be offered in *Women, Religion and the Christian Tradition* (LC Section E, 3.1a), which looks at women in the spiritual tradition; in *Issues of Justice and Peace* (LC Section F, 2.4b), which examines the just war tradition; and in *Worship, Prayer and Ritual* (LC Section G, 3.3), which offers honours students a study of the mystic tradition. One of the very demanding knowledge objectives of *Religion and Science* (LC Section J) is to 'be familiar with key moments in the relationship between science and theology from the renaissance to the present day'. There is no doubt about it: these two new syllabuses will stretch even the brightest pupils.

Those who argue for Religion to be examined in the Junior and Leaving Certificate examinations would normally favour the Academic model of RE. They would not, of course, be happy with a 'shallow' academic approach, where the emphasis is mainly on recall and simple understanding. They would look for a much 'deeper' academic approach, which insists on critical thinking skills as well. When the State examinations in RE are eventually held, one hopes that such critical skills will have been well learnt by Irish pupils: the NCCA syllabuses explicitly aim at developing not just knowledge, and not just understanding, but also the necessary skills to achieve religious literacy.[14] The people who object most strongly to the Academic approach to teaching Religion in school often pose the question, 'Is the personal aspect of religion not in danger of being lost?' (This question will be examined in more detail in Chapter 3).

In terms of *fundamental educational principles*, those who subscribe to the Educational Technology model of RE are probably people who like *precision* in everything. They admire the precision of research, science, technology, the law and poetry. Accordingly, they don't always see eye to eye with those who use the Open Education model. The Open model, they claim, leaves too much to chance. It tends to make all religious education very 'airy fairy'. That is why the advocates of Educational Technology place such emphasis on the importance of having clear aims and objectives in one's teaching.

The Bachelor of Religious Education degree course in the Mater Dei Institute emphasises this perspective, through the programme of teaching strategies and meta-strategies that has been developed there by the Education Department. Both the New Zealand Religious Education programme and the NCCA syllabuses are also clearly influenced by the Educational Technology model.[15] They assume that, unless one shapes one's teaching in terms of clear aims and objectives, one will never know to what extent one has taught successfully. If religion can be described with a certain degree of precision, then a major *aim* of religious education is to use teaching strategies that facilitate the growth of detailed and systematic religious understanding. In trying to bring about such precise knowledge and understanding, it is essential to praise and encourage the pupils.

Of course, this desire for precision and strategic planning can mean that there is little room for the unexpected in teaching. The Educational Technology model, when pushed to extremes, may exclude from the teaching process the answer from a pupil that sheds new light on an old idea, the new images made possible in a less structured teaching environment, and the role of lateral thinking in the generation of new insights.

The Social Reconstructionists have probably read Paulo Freire, the great Brazilian educationist. They will, no doubt, be well versed in the great social encyclicals such as *Peace on Earth, The Development of Peoples, Human Labour, The Social Concern of the Church*. The Vatican II document on the *Church in the Modern World* will probably be at their bedside. They will be aware that social justice, as a constitutive element of preaching the Gospel, has been a common theme in the official teaching of the Church in recent years. For them, the *fundamental principle*, the thing that really matters in religion, is that believers become apostles of *social justice*, in virtue of their baptism into the prophetic ministry of Christ.[16]

Those who favour this approach to teaching Religion are well catered for in the NCCA syllabuses, especially at Leaving Certificate level. This should not surprise us. The issues of social justice are very complex, and require of pupils a certain minimum of life experience and an ability to analyse social reality. At Junior level, however, some foundational work on social issues is clearly envisaged. Pupils will be invited (in *Communities of Faith*, JC Section A, 1) to study 'community breakdown'; and they will also examine (in JC Section F, 4) the concepts of 'stewardship, respect and integrity'. They will also be enabled to relate these social themes to 'the kingdom of God as preached by Jesus' (JC Section B, 3).

Much more detailed work on social justice will flow from *Christianity; Origins and Contemporary Expressions* (LC Section B, 2.4b) which examines the characteristics of the reign of God as preached by Jesus: namely, peace, inclusion, sharing of goods and a God of the powerless. In *Moral Decision-Making* (LC Section D, 4.3b), pupils will be invited to examine political and economic questions, violence, and crime and punishment. LC Section E, 2.4b will look at women's experience of exclusion and oppression; and 3.1c will explore women as social reformers. *Issues of Justice and Peace* (LC Section F, 1.2) will call for social analysis in terms of hunger, poverty and discrimination. *The Bible; Literature and Sacred Text* (LC Section H, 1.1d) will consider the influence of biblical insights on the Human Rights Charter; and part 4 will study some major Jewish prophets.

Social Reconstructionists understand religion in a slightly different way to the Academics. Instead of seeing religion as coming from the past into the present, they imagine it as coming from the future into the present. Christians are attracted by the future that God holds out to them, namely, God's *Kingdom*. In the light of that vision they want to work actively to change society for the better.[17] The *aim* of religious education is to produce Christian change agents,[18] to fashion 'shapers or architects of culture'.[19] More and more Religion teachers today have become quite at ease with this approach. However, those who are less sympathetic to it often ask, 'How feasible is such a project with pupils in school?' Or, alternatively, they might ask, 'Is this approach not putting the cart (social action) before the horse (the life of faith)?'[20]

Teachers and pupils

Having tasted the flavours of each model – at least insofar as *first principles* and *aims* are concerned – it is time now to examine the different images of *teachers* and *pupils* in each of the four models. The *pupil* in Open Education is ideally an active, searching, discovering person. Consequently, the *teacher* is the one who guides that journey of discovery. The teacher is a helper, the one who facilitates the pupil's religious development, almost like the Gaelic *anam-chara*. Here, teaching thrives on dialogue, and resists all imposition; it is a form of 'courtship' rather than 'custody'.[21]

Matters are slightly different in the Academic model. Here the ideal *pupil* is one who has fully understood the tradition and is both willing and able to play an individual part in passing on the riches of that tradition in modern idiom. Obviously, for pupils like that to emerge, one requires scholarly *teachers*, men and women well versed in educational, theological and cultural studies.

In the Educational Technology model, *teacher* and *pupils* relate almost as doctor and patients. Planning starts 'at the end'. The doctor identifies what needs to be put right in the patients' understanding of Religion, and then plans educational strategies to bring about suitable changes in the pupils (these strategies are like prescriptions). And, finally, the doctor arranges for a check-up later on, at which to evaluate both the patients' progress and the usefulness of the prescription.[22]

Those who work within the Social Reconstruction model recognise that many of history's greatest *teachers* have not been school teachers, but rather people of profound prophetic insight and sensitivity to issues of justice and peace in the world at large.[23] The whole world has been their classroom; and their *pupils* have been all those generous men and women of every culture, creed and class who are prepared to sacrifice themselves in the interests of justice, peace and harmony on earth. Working within this model are those who tend to view adult education as the key to future developments in religious education. In applying these insights to the more confined field of school teaching, many interesting proposals, such as the *Ballygall Project*,[24] have tried to put before pupils during school hours a range of practical challenges in the local community which, upon reflection, can lead to new learning.

Curriculum and ethos

In any discussion of education, the issue of *curriculum* figures very prominently. For years the education system of the USSR was unashamedly geared towards moulding all its citizens into the perfect Communist State. In the USA, a major aspiration of the public education system has been to produce people who are democrats at heart. In many countries, if a new social or economic problem arises, e.g. AIDS or mass unemployment, there is a strong call for schools to do something to rectify the situation by, for example, introducing a new subject on the curriculum.

Social Reconstructionists stress the social and ethical issues of the day, from a Christian perspective. These issues and this perspective would provide the content or substance of their *curriculum*. But equally important would be the process whereby the curriculum would be implemented, namely, the active involvement of teacher and pupil in trying to solve the problems in the light of Christ. There would be a certain flexibility or unpredictability about the content here, because issues would be changing from year to year. A similar flexibility of content is also to be seen in the *curriculum* drawn up by Open Educationists, because they always try to build the curriculum around the needs, questions, interests and experiences of their pupils.

On the other hand, the content of *curricula* produced in the other two models (Academic and Educational Technology) would be more predictable, and also more systematic. In the case of the Academic model, current theological writings would usually shape the content.[25] Teachers following such a *curriculum* would help pupils develop an academic interest in Religion and might even identify future Religion teachers or budding theologians.

A new approach to curriculum development has recently been pioneered by the Italian State through its introduction into primary schools of a religious studies programme, justified not in terms of religion or theology, but in terms of the cultural impact of the Catholic religion in Italian society. The NCCA's new RE syllabuses also justify themselves on educational rather than on narrowly religious or theological grounds. Hence there is content from not only Christian theology but also from other religions, philosophy, sociology, history and from science. Of course, one has to ask, 'Is systematic study of this rich and varied content really feasible within the constraints of school classrooms today?' A positive answer to this question has been given by the 'Scope and Sequence Chart' of the New Zealand National Syllabus, *Understanding Faith*. A broadly similar systematic approach is central to the *curricula* produced by Educational Technologists, who emphasise that learning objectives be achieved in a proper logical sequence.[26]

The Catholic School talks about 'the outlook on life that permeates the school'(32). This is sometimes referred to as the *ethos* of the school. Because of the critical assumptions of Social Reconstructionists, they always stress the need for creating a just society within the school environment as a prerequisite for developing pupils capable of moving on into the larger political area of social justice.[27] The recent debate on education in Ireland has seen many exciting new proposals for life in schools. Among these was a recommendation that Student Representative Councils be set up in second-level schools. The hope implicit in such a proposal is that pupils would learn to take responsible control of their lives as they grow to maturity.

The *ethos* of a school operating out of the Academic model would obviously be one that stressed intellectual standards, that encouraged serious study and put a premium on the critical faculties of insight, reasoning and communicating the truth. In a school based on the Open Education model, the key-note of the *atmosphere* would be acceptance of the worth of all the pupils, especially those incapable of serious study. While scholarly achievement would be highly prized among the pupils, the Open approach would stress that 'it is not the task of *every Christian* to reinterpret the faith for each generation, or even for themselves. To begin with, many people are simply incapable of that'.[28] In the Open approach, the 'heart' of religion would be more central than the 'head' of religion, as happens in the Academic and

Educational Technology models. In this latter model, everything about the school, from classroom to library to assembly points to play-grounds, would be carefully organised and planned so as to maximise the efforts of the teaching staff in bringing about the carefully chosen change-objectives in the lives of the pupils.

Evaluation or Assessment

Evaluation is a key aspect of education.[29] The distinctive quality of different views of teaching usually becomes evident when one examines the purpose of evaluation or *assessment*. What are teachers trying to assess? Is it their pupils' ability to answer set questions? (the normal examination grading system, typical of the traditional Academic model). Or are teachers evaluating how well the pupils have achieved precise understanding in response to strategic teaching? (the Educational Technology model). Or is evaluation more comprehensive, asking how do schools function in society, and how might they function; how much can schools be expected to achieve in bringing about social change; and would pupils be convicted, by their actions, of being Christian? (the Social Reconstruction model). A brief look at the assessment procedures proposed for the new NCCA syllabuses reveals that 'personal faith commitment and/or affiliation to a particular religious grouping'[30] is never meant to be assessed. The only valid matter for assessment is knowledge, understanding, skills and attitudes. The modes of assessment are final written examination, as well as journal work, followed by an individual interview.

In each of these kinds of evaluation, an attempt is made to achieve a certain objectivity. But, by its very nature, the Open Education approach tends more towards subjective assessment. Rather than asking, 'Has Joe reached grade A or a satisfactory grade common to most others?', it enquires, 'Has Joe done as well as he might?'

Conclusion

In this chapter I have outlined four distinct approaches to Religion teaching. No teacher is likely to be an absolute purist in implementing these models. But most teachers can probably recognise themselves and their colleagues in these models. Though examination syllabuses, such as those developed by the NCCA, are obviously closest to the heart of the teachers who subscribe to the Academic model, my analysis also reveals that all other kinds of Religion teachers are catered for by different elements and various emphases in the new syllabuses. Each distinct approach is valued and each kind of Religion teacher is valued. Hopefully this can lead to greater co-operation in the teaching of Religion.

Notes

1. R. Newton, 'Four models of teaching religion', in Our Sunday Visitor, *PACE* 11 (1982).

2. G. Rossiter, 'Diversity in curriculum in RE in Catholic Schools in Australia', in Christian Education Movement, *British Journal of Religious Education* (Spring 1982), p. 88. See also R. C. Miller (ed.), *Theologies of Religious Education.*

3. A. Thatcher, 'A Critique of Inwardness in RE', *BJRE* 14 (1), 1991, pp. 22-27; and a response from D. Hay and J. Hammond, 'When you pray, Go to your Private Room', *BJRE* 14 (3), 1992, pp. 145-150.

4. P. M. Devitt, *TYMB*, pp. 84-92.

5. This is how I shall refer to the text of the *Junior Certificate Religious Education syllabus*: 'JC Section D, 2 and 3' means *Junior Certificate*, Section D, Parts 2 and 3.

6. 'LC Section A, 2.2' means the RE syllabus for Leaving Certificate (LC), *Section A , Part 2, sub-section 2.*

7. R. Reichert, *A Learning Process for Religious Education;* see also a summary of Reichert's model in P. M. Devitt, *TYMB,* pp. 93-102; and G. Moran, *God Still Speaks,* chapter 4.

8. See Hogan and Williams (eds.), *FRIE*, where A. Walsh describes the task of religious education as 'one of clearing the debris, removing the obstacles and allowing the innate urge towards the transcendent to emerge' (p. 73).

9. T. Quinlan, 'What Future for Religious Education?', *The Furrow* (Feb. 1996), p. 101.

10. In recent years the academic approach to RE has been well described by M. Crawford and G. Rossiter, *Missionaries to a Teenage Culture;* by the Vatican document, *RDECS,* par. 90; and by the Aotearoa/ New Zealand syllabus, *Understanding Faith.*

11. For an account of 'Instruction as Religious Education', see P. M. Devitt, 'Religious Education', in M. Glazier and M. K. Hellwig (eds.), *The Modern Catholic Encyclopedia*, pp. 731-734.

12. See A. R. Gobbel, 'Christian Education with adolescents: An invitation to thinking', in United States Catholic Conference, *The Living Light* (Summer 1980).

13. T. Groome, *Christian Religious Education*, Ch. 7, 'A Way of Knowing'. For a summary of Groome's approach, see P. M. Devitt, *TYMB*, pp. 102-110.

14. *Junior Certificate Religious Education Syllabus*, p. 46.

15. See Aotearoa/New Zealand Catholic Bishops' Conference, *Understanding Faith, Syllabus Document*, pp. 4-7; the JC syllabus *passim*; and the LC draft syllabus, pp. 38-39.

16. See Sacred Congregation for Catholic Education, *RDECS*, par. 45.

17. See G. Boran, *The Pastoral Challenges of a New Age*, p. 138, for an account of a very similar approach, called 'the Transforming Inductive Model'.

18. See J. Elias, 'RE for power and liberation', in *LL* (1976, no.1); and D. W. Gooderham, 'Dialogue and Emancipation', *BJRE* (Spring 1983).

19. T. Larkin, *FRIE*, p. 103.

20. With his usual wit, C. S. Lewis reminds us that 'nothing but the courage and unselfishness of individuals is ever going to make any system work properly'. See *Mere Christianity*, p. 67.

21. P. Hogan, *The Custody and Courtship of Experience*, pp. 168-9.

22. M. Chater, 'A Healing Model of RE', *BJRE* 17 (2), 1995, pp. 121-128 offers an interesting version of this approach.

23. See J. A. Grassi, *Jesus as Teacher*.

24. L. S. McCarthy, *Creating Space for RE. The Ballygall Project: Theory and Practice*.

25. See J. Astley, 'Theology and Curriculum Selection', *BJRE* 10 (2), 1988, pp. 86-91.

26. For a fuller, more nuanced treatment of this topic, see J. M. Lee, 'The Authentic Source of Religious Instruction', in N. Thompson (ed.), *Religious Education and Theology*.

27. See J. Callaghan and M. Cockett, *Are Our Schools Christian?*; and

G. Rossiter, *LL* (1981, no.2), 'The gap between aims and practice in RE in Catholic schools'.

28. See J. Astley, *The Philosophy of Christian Religious Education*, p. 103.

29. See M. Bezzina, P. Chesterton, K. Johnston and S. Sanber, 'Evaluation Practices in RE: A Sydney Study', *BJRE* 16 (2), Spring 1994, pp. 102-113.

30. *Junior Certificate Religious Education Syllabus*, p. 45.

Chapter 2

HOW DO DIFFERENT TEACHERS TEACH MORALITY?

One of the most remarkable comments made about the early Christian communities by observant outsiders was, 'See how these Christians love one another!' These observers were clearly impressed by the quality of Christian love.[1] Even though these outsiders may not have sensed the divine source of this love (Christian disciples can love *only* with God's love and *only* because God has first loved them), they could see clearly how Christian faith was affecting the moral life of believers.[2] And, of course, Christian faith is meant to do just that. A living Christian faith should express itself in a life of love. Christians, according to St James, should be 'doers of the word, and not hearers only' (Jm 1:22). One's Christian faith should give substance to one's moral values and shape one's major and minor life decisions. In another work, I have described the ecology of Christian morality in these terms: the Spirit of God is the religious *foundation* of Christian morality; Christian morality then takes a sacramental and community *shape*, generates the radical process known as conversion (*metanoia*), and merits the *name* of love (*agape*).[3]

The fact that outsiders, many of whom may not have been religious people themselves, could both recognise and treasure the love lived by Christians, proves that morality has a wider constituency than religion. There have been, and always will be, many people who, in spite of their sharing in no religious faith community, will nevertheless aspire to be moral. The moral vocation is not confined to religious people. It is a calling responded to by humans of every religion and of none. Such is the clear assumption of the moral components of the two new RE syllabuses. In fact, the first aim of the Junior Certificate Section F (*The Moral Challenge*) is 'to explore the human need to order relationships at the personal, communal and global levels' (p. 38). Here is a recognition that humans relate at many different levels. And so, morality is concerned with the question, how should these relationships be properly ordered so that all people can live a good human life?

Having situated morality at the heart of the human relational enterprise, the Junior Certificate syllabus then encourages the early adolescents to take stock of the range of influences that have shaped their moral life so far, 'such as home, peer group, school, state, religion etc.' (p. 40). The importance of moral codes and moral principles is stressed, but even more so is the 'moral vision' that inspires them. 'Authority and tradition' are not the favourite words of young people; and yet their 'wisdom' is unashamedly acknowledged. Recognising that young adolescents are trying to take the first steps in their autonomous moral journey, the syllabus then deals with 'growing in morality' (Part 3, p. 41). It encourages the process of 'moral development from selfishness to altruism'. It links conscience formation with growing 'moral maturity'. Part 4 (p. 42) is perhaps the most imaginative of the entire Section. It examines 'the process of moral decision-making', but does so in the context of 'two different religious moral visions'. The overall aim here is 'to explore the moral visions of two major world religions, one of which should be Christianity' (p. 38). This may sound very demanding, but the approach is very practical: it analyses the impact of these visions on the lives of people by 'considering some current moral issues' (p. 38). The reality of 'moral failure' and the possibility of reconciliation ('the restoration of relationships') are both adverted to (p. 42).

The human search for moral value is explored in even more detail through the Leaving Certificate Section D (*Moral Decision-Making*). The first topic here is Thinking about Morality, which examines such issues as good and evil, personal and communal values, individual rights and the common good. These themes are a human inheritance available to all and sundry. They are elements in the grammar of morality. It is only in the context of presenting this moral grammar that the syllabus dares to develop a detailed moral *vocabulary* or 'word-store'. To achieve this, it examines the relationship between morality and religion, and identifies especially the specific riches of Christian moral thinking. It shows how Christian morality, based on the Jewish idea of covenant, and inspired by the vision of Jesus regarding justice and love, has been developed by various Christian traditions for almost two thousand years.[4] In particular, it emphasises the centrality of reconciliation as a Christian response to sin and moral depravity; it also examines the relationship between personal and social sin and introduces the concept of structural injustice. But this rich treatment of Christian morality is situated clearly within the context of, and in *dialogue* with, two other religious traditions, as well as the many moral principles and theories that abound in the pluralistic culture of today. The moral insights from all these diverse sources are equally treasured by the syllabus.

There is also a very *practical* aspect to the syllabus' treatment of Moral Decision-Making. While assuming a certain intellectual ability in pupils, the syllabus does not subscribe to an overly intellectual view of morality, as espoused by Lawrence Kohlberg. 'One need not be a moral philosopher in order to be a moral person.'[5] In a person's growth towards moral maturity, many factors other than intellect are influential: one's family and friends, one's religion and personal psychology. Human freedom has to be sculpted out of many raw materials. Furthermore, one's moral decisions are never made in the abstract but always relate to concrete challenges in every aspect of human living. Nor are the decisions arrived at easily, since alternative proposals are screaming at one from the wide range of ethical value systems deeply imbedded in modern culture. Many attractive voices are calling one this way and that. The syllabus alerts the pupils to these voices and encourages them to dialogue with them.

In short, the Leaving Certificate syllabus presents morality as a *human* search for life values. This common human search has a special tone within each specific religious community and yet takes place in a pluralist world of both common and competing value systems. The syllabus is convinced that ongoing dialogue is necessary in order that full moral truth will be discovered. Its perspective is very close to that of Gabriel Moran, who stressed the importance of listening to the voice of the great mystics: 'My contention is that the morality of mature people, an educational morality, must include an element of the mystical.'[6] The Leaving Certificate syllabus also seems to resonate with Donal Murray, who maintains that the search for moral truth must respect divergent voices.[7] He adds, however, that such respect and dialogue should not lapse into 'passive tolerance'.[8]

If such dialogue is so central to moral reflection, then a certain dialogue must first occur among the Religion teachers themselves. In Chapter 1, I discussed Newton's four models or styles of teaching. My contention now is that these different styles of teaching will inevitably give rise to different moral voices. In an attempt to encourage an open forum, and to allow these voices enough room to speak, I shall offer two apologias (one for the Open Education model, the other for the Educational Technology model). These will be supplemented by an imaginary 'Letter to the Editor' (regarding the Academic model) and an imaginary advertisement for a teacher versed in the Social Reconstruction model.

OPEN EDUCATION: An Apologia

'When I think of morality I immediately think of interpersonal relationships. Only human beings can have such relationships. It makes no sense to talk about the moral standards of monkeys. Only human persons can be moral. The aim of moral education is to help them become the free and responsible people they are capable of becoming.

As a teacher, I recognise that my pupils are growing and that their personalities are developing all the time.[9] Their entire life is like a journey. I am with them as a guide only for a part of that journey. I have to find out three things: (1) at what stage of the journey of life are they now moving? (2) what experience of life have they had before they met me? (3) how can I direct their development so that they will advance rather than regress in their moral thinking?

As a person who has already grown up (to some extent), I recognise that taking hold of my own destiny and deciding where I want to go in life has been central to my own moral development. Being free and responsible, I have searched for values that make sense of life and have tried to live these values from day to day. I should like my pupils to become more free and responsible and so discover their own moral values in their own personal way. I believe I can help them here because I have already walked the way they must go.

I place great emphasis, within education, on the ability of people to reflect on their experience of life. This ability increases as people grow up; but everyone has it to some extent, even if they can't articulate the contents of their reflections. In moral matters people can recognise how they have been truthful or careless, or how others have cared for them or insulted them or wronged them. As a teacher, I have to help my pupils in this task of recognising morality in life, and also in their task of understanding it and talking about it with others. As a Christian teacher, I believe that God is present within all people in the depths of their being, and that God is somehow experienced when people learn to care for each other and forgive each other. What most people recognise as the voice of conscience has an even deeper meaning for me, because I hear God calling in the voice of conscience.

Life is untidy. My pupils (and myself) have many unanswered questions, many unsatisfied needs. But, somehow, God is there in the confusion, waiting to be encountered. That's why I take such great care in coming to understand and to appreciate the interests and experiences of my pupils. I do this because I recognise that it is there that God is addressing a word to them and calling them out into the rich pastures of adult life. I need to be able to help my pupils hear and pay heed to that interior voice.

I'd like to be able to organise my work, but I find that very hard to do. There's a certain unpredictability about growth and about the way God's challenge echoes in people's hearts. My programme of moral education is quite flexible. It has to be. I must be relevant and must take my pupils' starting point quite seriously. They may not yet be ready to walk where I have been or to see things the way I see them.

At the end of each year I notice that some pupils have advanced more than others. Some don't seem to have learned anything. I hope I haven't turned the clock back for anybody, but that is always a possibility. Because I am more interested in the growth of individuals, I don't feel the need to set examinations. Examinations inevitably force me to compare this one with that one; but I prefer to see each pupil as unique and don't see the value of trying to find out if one is better or worse, more knowledgeable or ignorant than the others.

My basic philosophy of life is one of hope. Because I believe in God, I can afford to believe in people. I am hopeful that my pupils will leave me, better able to cope with the complexities of moral living than when we first met. I always try to express my hope in them by accepting them as they are (warts and all), by affirming their goodness and providing them with a stimulating environment within which to grow and mature.'

ACADEMIC MODEL: LETTER TO THE EDITOR

'Dear Sir,

In your columns recently I read that Religious Education is soon to be introduced as an examination subject in second-level schools and that pupils may take it at Junior Certificate (and eventually at Leaving Certificate) level. May I add my voice to the considerable debate that is now taking place.

This move is to be highly recommended. The world we live in is fast becoming a den of iniquity. Immorality and injustice are the order of the day. People don't seem to know the difference between right and wrong. And is it any wonder, when you think of the kind of play-acting that often passes for education? In the name of freedom, everything seems to be allowed nowadays. It may be fashionable to say that pupils have to be allowed to search for the truth, but I believe it is more important that they find a code of behaviour that will help them become better people and better citizens.

There is no substitute for diligent study. If young people are ever to know what is right and what is wrong, then they must be asked to work hard. I assume that the syllabuses will require them to study the moral precepts of Moses and that they will be introduced to the social teachings of the great Jewish prophets. I assume, furthermore, since many people here are Christians, that the moral teaching of Jesus (especially his Sermon on the Mount) and of St Paul will be carefully studied by every student.[10] There will obviously have to be some selectivity regarding the whole range of Christian moral teaching down to this day, but perhaps choices of content could be centred on such major topical issues as war, injustice, abortion, capital punishment, divorce, environmental pollution, child abuse, bribery and corruption, etc. Pupils today need to know how faithful people in the past coped with these and other moral issues. Without such basic knowledge, no pupil today should be regarded as morally educated.

I am not advocating that pupils be stuffed with items of knowledge culled from the past and from present scholarship. I appreciate that education must involve an ability to comprehend what is known and critically to evaluate it according to the situation of today's world. It's not enough, for example, to know that the attitudes of Christians towards warfare have changed down through the ages. Pupils should also be able to say *why* such changes took place and, furthermore, should be able to see the perennial value of 'peace-making' within the Christian life.

If the syllabuses are to be successful, then nobody should teach them who has not achieved a basic level of certified competence in moral philosophy, moral theology and Church/religious history. Since many teachers who do not have such qualifications may wish to be involved in moral education, it is imperative that the Department of Education sponsor whatever in-career courses may be required to qualify their teachers adequately. Justice would seem to require that the teachers in question should not have to pay the cost of these courses. Rather, they might even be given some extra financial incentives to encourage them to participate.

In English, Irish, French and other modern languages, it is now common to study some of the more outstanding literary figures of recent times. Is it too much to hope for that the great moral philosophers and moral theologians of the twentieth century would be explained to our young people today, so that they, in their turn, can creatively transmit to further generations the rich moral heritage that is ours?

There is an intellectual content in morality, since we must think and reason morally if we are to survive as human beings. I believe a challenging examination system will provide just the motivation that is needed for the young people of today to know, understand and assimilate the moral insights of humanity, of the great world religions and of the Churches. And, what is of even greater significance, it will surely unearth the hidden talents that will one day become the moral teachers of the future.'

I remain,
Yours truly,
Catherine Court.

EDUCATIONAL TECHNOLOGY: AN APOLOGIA

'I have grave reservations about the approaches of certain teachers to moral education. I refer to those who talk about pupils' finding themselves through discussion, or discovering God in the mysteries of life. This is all too vague for me. It may be a lovely theory but, in practice, it doesn't and, I believe, cannot work. Believe me, I have nothing against the theory except that it doesn't work. I have watched teachers try it out. I have tried it out myself. But always the same – disaster or, at the very least, total confusion. Many of these discussions that were supposed to yield deeper insights into morality have been no more than a sharing of mutual ignorance. They have reminded me of a group of pups chasing their own tails round and round in circles, and regularly having a bite at some other pup's tail, while the so-called teacher sat and grinned and passed it all off as youthful enthusiasm or lack of experience.[11]

And then one day I heard of the teacher who was happy that his pupils had found God in Hare Krishna. And he told me the story of an Indian Jesuit priest who was not at all embarrassed when he learned that the guiding lights in the local Communist party were all his ex-pupils. How can people feel they have succeeded as moral educators if their pupils adopt moral principles that are manifestly at variance with standard Christian teaching and practice? No amount of talking and discussing will ever lead pupils to a clear, precise grasp of moral truth. Moral righteousness has an objective character. It is not something we invent from our subconscious. It is a given, an absolute. And it has been spelt out so often in the past that all one needs is to be confronted with it so as to be challenged by it and, hopefully, be changed by it.

Moses expounded objective moral standards for the chosen people. He left us the moral law we call the Ten Commandments. Jesus took these a stage further; but he never did away with them. We are, therefore, in a position to describe with reasonable accuracy and clarity what a moral person would be within the Jewish-Christian tradition we belong to. She would honour God and her parents, would not commit adultery or steal. She would be honest and would not be in any way avaricious. She would be a caring, loving, peace-making, forgiving person. This is what a moral person would look like, if she were Jewish or Christian. She wouldn't just know all the theories about justice and love and forgiveness. She would put them into practice in her life and could be seen to be doing the truth.

Given that this is what the ideal moral person looks like, and since real people are far from the ideal, they would have to change greatly in the course of life. Jesus recognised this when he called on people to be converted, to have a change of heart – he meant them to live differently, according to his standards and values. Moral education is, therefore, faced with the task of helping people to change their behaviour, their attitudes and their values. Knowing what the values, standards and behaviours are is not enough. It's essential to live them in action. Otherwise our learning is just "head-learning". It needs to be "heart-learning" as well.

Some people have an image of the moral educator as a scholar versed in moral theology and moral philosophy. Others think of the moral educator as a kind of spiritual director, schooled in Rogerian non-judgmental counselling. I prefer to think of the moral educator as a doctor. Just like the medical practitioner, the moral educator is confronted with people who, though reasonably healthy, yet have health problems. Like the doctor, the moral educator has the task of prescribing the remedies in terms of class-input and student activity. After all, one becomes honest only by doing honest actions.

But, most important of all, teachers of morality must be able to evaluate critically the outcome of their input and prescribed activities. If they are successful (meaning the pupils are closer to the moral ideal after taking their courses than they were beforehand), then they have cause for satisfaction. If they fail, then they had better reconsider their whole teaching strategy. Maybe their short-term objectives are not

suitable for the particular students they are teaching. Then they need
to be refined, without prejudice, however, to their long-term objective
of producing pupils who are clearly and recognisably Christian in
behaviour.

Talk of strategy here reminds me that the moral educator is not
only like a doctor. The moral educator is also like a military general.
The warfare is the constant one between good and evil, between light
and darkness. The pupils are the infantry. The moral educator is their
leader and, as such, is constantly setting definable and achievable
targets for them to achieve. Unless the strategy adopted by the moral
educator takes into account the real world in which the pupils live, it
will be worthless, because irrelevant. Unless the strategy takes into
account the reality of the pupils, then it will not succeed as far as they
are concerned. And if the teaching, no matter how well articulated or
how beautifully presented and argued for, still fails to bring about the
kinds of changes in the pupils that show they are winning the battle
for good – then that teacher has failed. The teacher may have been
aiming at the good, but unless the pupils reach the good, then the
teacher has failed.

Planning one's work as a moral educator means beginning at the
end. It means asking, "Where are my pupils going? What are the
obstacles in their way? How can I help them to overcome these
obstacles and so arrive at their goal?" I need to identify the likely
sequence of obstacles, so they can be realistically approached and
surmounted. As a practical measure, I need to plan carefully, so that at
every class period they will achieve some verifiable behavioural
objective. Any scheme of work must include regular opportunities for
evaluating how far along the road to righteousness my pupils have
walked with me. Without this evaluation I cannot know if they are
learning anything from me, and if they are not learning, then I am not
really teaching.'[12]

THE SOCIAL RECONSTRUCTION MODEL:
An Advertisement

The Board of Management of St Patrick's Community School invites applications for the post of **Teacher of Macro-Morality**. This is a new post, which has been created to meet the demands of the new Junior Certificate syllabus of Religious Education that will be offered here, commencing September 2001. The post is full-time and incremental. St Patrick's is an equal opportunity employer.

Candidates should have a recognised degree which involves a major study of Micro-Morality (the morality of interpersonal and familial relationships). They will also be required to demonstrate an adequate appreciation of the complexity of Macro-Morality (the morality of relationships between groups within society and between nations). Practical experience of working for improvements in the social fabric of Irish society will be of considerable advantage to all prospective candidates.

Upon appointment, the **Teacher of Macro-Morality** will be expected to plan such courses of study and organise such practical work within the local community as will gradually transform the pupils into workers for social justice. As the pupils learn to become agents of social change for the better (in keeping with the vision of Mahatma Gandhi, Martin Luther King and the Vatican Council document on *The Church in the Modern World)*, the **Teacher of Macro-Morality** will constantly evaluate the hidden curriculum of St Patrick's Community School (in close liaison with the Chaplain, the Religion teachers, the Counsellor, the Principal and the Staff Association) and will propose changes aimed at making this school a more just society.

The **Teacher of Macro-Morality** will offer courses to prepare pupils adequately to cope with the Junior Certificate examination, as well as practical field-work both within and outside the school to prepare pupils to take a positive and creative role in the reconstruction of Irish society, according to principles of justice and peace. Given the complex theoretic-practical nature of the proposed course, candidates will be required to demonstrate a variety of teaching skills, ranging from lecture to discussion to problem-solving to field-work to conducting social analysis. An ability to assess the progress of individual students and to evaluate the success of the study programme will be essential.

Interviews will be held in St Patrick's on 1 April 2001 (weather permitting). Candidates for the post should forward a recent Curriculum Vitae, together with three references, to the Secretary of St Patrick's, Ireland's Eye, Howth, Co. Dublin, to arrive not later than 29 February 2001. The successful candidate will be offered a loan to purchase a boat.

Conclusion

The value of the moral component of the new RE syllabuses should now be clear. Junior Certificate pupils will be helped to grow from a childish morality, based largely on the expectations of significant others, to a more freely chosen morality, rooted in a challenging *moral vision*. Leaving Certificate pupils will be helped to learn the *grammar* of morality, as well as the specific moral *language* of their own religious or secular tradition. They will also be encouraged to take an active part in the *conversation* between different moral voices in the search for moral truth. Since both syllabuses allow teachers a *variety of pedagogical approaches* towards teaching the moral life, they will therefore provide a valid educational service for the young people of Ireland, a service somewhat akin to that provided by the study of European languages. I hope our Religion teachers will avail themselves of this service.

Notes

1. For a good exposition of 'Commitment and Discipleship in the New Testament' see the article of this title by U. Vanni, in J. S. Marino (ed.), *Biblical Themes in Religious Education.*

2. This idea is implicit in the very title of S. M. de Benedittis, *Teaching Faith and Morals.* See also the fine document by the Irish Bishops, entitled *Conscience.*

3. See P. M. Devitt, *ID*, Chapter 5, 'Changing Radically under the Spirit's Inspiration'.

4. For a good introduction to a specifically Christian view of morality and moral thinking, see C. Dykstra, *Vision and Character: A Christian Educator's Alternative to Kohlberg.*

5. *Ibid.,* p. 19.

6. See G. Moran, *No Ladder to the Sky: Education and Morality,* p. 61.

7. See D. Murray, 'Morality and Culture in Dialogue', in D. A. Lane (ed.), *RCD*, p. 229.

8. *Ibid.,* p. 219.

9. For a fine reflection on the need to integrate the doctrinal and moral dimensions of faith, and the importance of testing the insights from developmental psychology, see J. E. Greer, 'Moral and Religious Education: a Christian Approach', in L. Francis and A. Thatcher (eds.), *Christian Perspectives for Education*, pp. 329-339.

10. For some very helpful tips on understanding and presenting the moral section of the *CCC*, see K. Kelly, 'Life in Christ: The Moral Teaching of the Catechism of the Catholic Church' in *From a Parish Base: Essays in Moral and Pastoral Theology.*

11. For a more positive account of classroom discussion, see Greer, Harris and McElhinny, 'A Study of Classroom Discussion in RE', *BJRE* 12 (1), 1989, pp. 92-102. Groome recommends for every classroom a process he calls 'creating conversation'. He claims that, because 'conversation' is rooted in the essentially communal nature of human life, it can lead to the gradual discovery of moral truth. See T. Groome, *Educating for Life*, p. 203.

12. For a different approach to moral education, with an emphasis on helping those who 'limp rather than stride towards the moral ideal', see D. Harrington, 'Morality and the Catechism', in P. M. Devitt (ed.), *A Companion to the Catechism*, pp. 59-68.

Chapter 3

WHAT IS THE MAIN PURPOSE OF THE RELIGION CLASS?

The religious development of young people

The religious development of young people happens in many contexts, which are distinct, though complementary. It can take place at home, in the parish, with friends, at school, in the Religion class, through the media, etc. In most situations, the religious development is informal rather than formal, unprogrammed rather than planned, implicit rather than explicit, unpredictable rather than deliberate. If one fails to define clearly the influences on religious development within each context, there is a danger of having unrealistic expectations.

The religious character of the **home** is usually the most important influence on a child's religious faith. As the ceremony of Baptism states, parents are the first educators of their children in the ways of faith. Other home educators might be brothers, sisters, uncles, aunts, grandparents, in fact any member of the extended family. A person's religious identity is normally established within a household where religious faith is alive and strong. Most people become a Muslim or a Jew or a Protestant or a Catholic simply by being born into a particular household. It's like what happens in the learning of the mother tongue; it is caught, rather than taught. People almost grow into faith.

But notice the word *almost*. The analogy is not perfect. Since faith is a mysterious free response to God, faith cannot be programmed. There is nothing totally predictable about the process of handing on the faith in the home. For example, two children from the same family faith environment could grow up, one a believer and the other a non-believer. The children of practising parents could cease to practise at a certain age. Though most people probably retain the faith they were born into, and though many succeed in developing it further, many people also change their native faith. This happens very obviously in the case of those who convert to another religion (like Saul of Tarsus, or John Henry Newman, or Cat Stevens), but also less noticeably in the case of those who may never convert. Some such people can throw away or abandon the liturgical practice of their faith, while still retaining many of the beliefs and moral standards of their faith. At a very extreme level, some believers may even become enemies of the faith that once nourished them.

This analysis suggests that, while home is crucial, it is not everything. In regard to religious development, the home does not predetermine a child's faith. What the child ultimately believes in, and lives by, is often influenced by experiences outside the home. Hence the importance of such factors as the local parish, the friends one makes, the school one attends and, of course, many cultural factors such as television and radio. Any of these elements, either singly or jointly, might ultimately have even more influence on the religious development of a particular individual than the parents and immediate family. Here are some examples:

- Becoming part of a vibrant **parish** folk group or prayer circle could be the major element in the religious growth of Joe or Mary. Equally, their religious growth could be stifled through meeting an unsympathetic priest in confession.
- Children of parents who faithfully practise their religion may, at a certain age, respond to the contradictory behaviour pattern of their **friends** and cease religious practice altogether. Or it could sometimes work in reverse.
- Children from homes where the faith is weak can gain an insight into the riches of Christian life through meeting good Religion teachers and chaplains in school. Children from homes of strong faith can become weaker in the faith if their religious education in **school** does not challenge their minds and imaginations in the way other subjects do.
- Children of firm religious convictions can be shattered by some of the negative aspects of modern print **media**, radio and television. Children of underdeveloped religious sensitivity can have their religious spirit set alight by the way the media sometimes expose 'man's inhumanity to man'.

Within school

Schools can contribute in many ways to the religious development of children. The **school ethos**[1] or atmosphere can foster values such as care for the weak, co-operation between pupils, justice and fair play towards all, respect for truth, a passion for the environment, a love of learning and a respect for honest effort. Everybody in the school (from management, through principal, teachers and auxiliary staff to the newest pupil) either contributes to or detracts from the creation of this ethos. Religion teachers would help to foster this ethos, in the school in general as well as in the classrooms, but they certainly could not produce it on their own.

The school may have a **pastoral care programme**[2] to support its pupils on an individual basis. An alert Religion teacher would notice pupils in class who might benefit from this type of care. Such a teacher would be willing to take part, if required, in this pastoral care but, at the very least, would notify the personnel involved of the pupils in question, especially those who are known as 'deviants'.[3]

The school may have a **chaplaincy service** and may provide space for prayers, meditation, class Masses, Penance services and weekend retreats.[4] Many Religion teachers would contribute to this service, but they would not be the only teachers expected to do so.

The school may encourage the setting up of **outreach groups** that contribute to the local community. The Religion teacher might well be the inspiration of some of these groups, as happened with the Ballygall project;[5] but it could well be that other teachers are better equipped to organise such projects outside school hours.

The school may have **reminders** of a religious nature, such as crucifixes and paintings. The Religion teacher might be expected to comment critically on existing images and make suggestions for new ones.

The school may show its commitment to Religion by **employing** some graduates of the Mater Dei Institute of Education or Mount Oliver or Maynooth to teach Religion and co-ordinate the work of religious education. Especially now, with new examination syllabuses being introduced, the school may encourage some teachers of other subjects to do in-career courses to improve the quality of the Religion teaching they are asked to do. The professionally qualified, specialist teachers of Religion would normally be expected to help these other teachers from time to time through sharing ideas and resources.

In the spirit of *RDECS*, which calls on each Catholic school to 'have a set of educational goals which are distinctive'(100), the school may draw up a **policy statement** explaining its commitment to the religious development of all its pupils. It may set up structures within which school staff and parents of pupils might plan some aspects of school policy, e.g. the manner of implementation of the AIDS Education programme or the Relationships and Sexuality Education (RSE) programme. Religion teachers would normally contribute to the articulation and implementation of school policy relating to religious education, and would probably be among the teachers asked to help with specific programmes such as the AIDS or RSE programmes.

As will be shown in the Appendix, *RDECS* assumes that teachers of History, Music, Art, Science, Geography (in fact, almost any subject area) occasionally encounter moral or religious questions as they arise naturally in the course of their teaching (54-61). When this happens, the individual **teacher of a secular subject** can explore these questions briefly and so contribute to the religious development of the pupils. This is very like what Seamus Heaney called the 'education of the spirit' through poetry.[6] Sometimes, school policy will encourage forms of collaboration between teachers of secular subjects and teachers of Religion. When a Religion teacher is also a teacher of another subject, a kind of 'internal interdisciplinary collaboration' is both possible and valuable.

The school may foster the religious development of pupils by providing them with a **Religion room** and by making available to teachers adequate resources for the onerous task of teaching Religion. Religion teachers would indicate the resources that are available for purchasing.

The specific or unique contribution of classroom Religion teaching

The analysis so far has identified the many different ways in which a school can contribute to the religious development of its pupils.[7] Normally the Religion teacher will contribute to all facets of school life, as these bear on the religious development of pupils. Nevertheless, the Religion teacher will not be the only teacher or staff member to do so. It is very important to bear constantly in mind that, according to the vision of *RDECS*, the catechetical mission of the Religion teacher is a part only of the integral catechetical mission of the entire school.[8] Given this perspective, what then is the *specific* or *unique* contribution that the Religion teacher alone, in the confines of the Religion classroom, is supposed to make to the religious development of the pupils? The Australian authors Marisa Crawford and Graham Rossiter call it the provision of a challenging educational encounter with religion.[9]

Before clarifying this important concept, it is well to list a wide range of *possible* encounters with religion. A child growing up in a believing household encounters religion as part of ordinary, daily life. A person freely attending a Papal Mass encounters a dramatic facet of the Catholic religion; altogether different, at the level of encounter and experience, would be compulsory attendance at Sunday Mass or attendance simply in order not to offend one's parents or neighbours. When the Director of the Museum of Atheism (himself an atheist) met a religious sister in Moscow, this was his first encounter with a living nun, and this living encounter with religion gave him a new sense of religion as a possible way of life, rather than something just stored in museum exhibits. In the film, *Au revoir les enfants*, the welcome given the Jewish boy in a Catholic boarding school was, for him, a challenging encounter with another great world religion. Other valuable encounters with religion could be listening to the Angelus on RTÉ, or going on pilgrimage to the Holy Land, or visiting mosques, synagogues, old burial sites, holy wells, etc. Any of these encounters with religion may be educational, in the broad sense of being culturally and personally enriching. People may indeed learn something from the experience. But none of these encounters is primarily or deliberately or explicitly a teaching moment.

Different from these encounters with religion is the *'challenging educational encounter'*, which takes place in a very precise context, with an inbuilt and explicit teaching-learning dynamic: the school classroom. I propose to explore this idea now in two ways:

(1) Reflections deriving from the meaning of religion and faith-stance:

My assumptions here are twofold: *one*, that faith is a matter of taking a stand or a position in life; and, *two*, that people can 'stand back from' their stance in life, can 'move out of their skins', as it were, can 'bracket that commitment' for a while.[10] For a religious person, this means to distance oneself somewhat from one's life of religious faith, with a view to exploring its inner dynamic. This is not at all an easy manoeuvre, because it 'involves holding at arm's length what is most naturally and appropriately held in embrace'.[11] And what about non-believers, people who subscribe to no particular religious tradition? I assume here what many people today accept, namely, that all human beings are in some sense people of faith, though, of course, this may be a secular (or non-religious) faith.[12] If so, then such people can be helped in a Religion class to 'stand back from' their particular secular faith stance as well.

Within class in school, the Religion teacher is expected to 'wear many different hats' at different times, e. g. to be a teacher of Religion, to be a catechist, to be a carer of pupils and to be an agent of school discipline. But the Religion teacher's *specific* task is to help pupils learn to think about religious issues. Gabriel Moran claims that class-work in school is part of the broad activity of 'religious education' whenever it becomes 'a search for meaning in the explicit doctrines and practices of a particular religion'.[13] This search for religious meaning is a *specific* kind of encounter with religion. Parents and priests and friends may engage in catechesis, in other words, they may share faith and hand on the faith; so too may the school as a whole; but it is the *specific* task of the Religion teacher in the classroom to inform pupils about the richness of their religious tradition (*factual knowledge*) and to provide them with the skills and the encouragement they need to think deeply and seriously and with irony about religious issues in their own lives and also in the world of today (*systematic knowledge*). These are the major elements of the challenging educational encounter with religion. They constitute its 'investigative character'.[14]

All of this rather 'impersonal' or 'objective' knowledge (this 'standing back') can be explored in class no matter what level of faith or unbelief the pupils are at (no matter what *personal knowledge* they may have, in fact, no matter what their personal 'stance' may be), because what is being aimed at in the Religion class is knowledge, understanding and the skills to pursue independent thinking in Religion.[15] These are the aims that every subject in school should have. They are, therefore, suitable aims for classroom Religion teaching.[16] The Religion teacher will be glad to note that the Junior Certificate RE syllabus provides in each Section, as well as overall aims and objectives, a detailed list of 'key concepts' and a 'description of content'. A similar teaching-learning dynamic is also tangible in the proposed Leaving Certificate RE syllabus, which outlines, in each Section, the precise knowledge, understanding, skills and attitudes that are to be sought in the Religion class.

By seeking these objectives, the Religion teacher is encouraging pupils to become 'religiate'[17] (a notion analogous to 'literate' and 'numerate'). The teacher is not *directly* encouraging their 'religious' life. But, if pupils have religious convictions, then these could perhaps begin to change from beliefs of convention to beliefs of intention. For those who have no firm religious conviction, this kind of Religion teaching and learning would be an exercise in empathy with those who have such convictions.[18]

The Mater Dei Institute of Education provides an analogy of what I have said so far. When, for example, a priest lecturer celebrates Mass in the oratory there, he assumes that the students and staff are present as believers and he appeals directly to their faith. When the chaplain organises retreats in Manresa, or when he meets students in his room, he assumes that personal faith development is on the agenda. The students' encounter with religion in these contexts is, ideally, a total encounter, and so, potentially, a richer encounter than what happens at lectures. But, when the lecturer in Religious Studies gives a course, she talks in such a way as to communicate information the students may not have, and to spark off their thinking so that they can come to understand what religion means. If what she says occasionally helps the spiritual growth or faith commitment of an individual student, that is an added bonus. In such a case, the experience of a good lecture may prove to be, for that student, as rich an encounter with religion as even a retreat or the Mass. A lecturer would certainly welcome this *indirect* outcome, but it is not something she would primarily aim at in the lecture course.

This is how it should be for the Religion teacher in class in school. One should aim for knowledge, understanding and skills of enquiry, and leave the rest to God. God will surely, in God's own mysterious manner, find ways for the knowledge and the learning to contribute to the maturing faith of young people. Thomas Groome sees a probable link between teaching Religion and deeper personal faith. He argues for 'a rigorous academic study as an aid to deepening one's faith' and for teaching 'religiously in a way that is thoroughly educational and yet likely to form people's faith identity'.[19] I would suggest here a softening of language, and talk of a 'possible' rather than a 'probable' link. In other words, if the Religion teacher aims for knowledge, then a deepening faith life may well come, but always as a surprise. On the other hand, if she should aim in the classroom *directly* for faith development or spiritual growth in pupils, nothing at all may take place. In teaching, as in human life, many good things happen, not because teachers have aimed at them, but rather in spite of the fact that they have sought them out.[20]

Patrick S. Fahy's research into the religious effectiveness of Australian Catholic schools proves that the school is a 'significant predictor of student's Christian faith'.[21] From this he concludes that he has scotched the claim made by Crawford and Rossiter that faith sharing and faith development are best left to the out-of-classroom arena. Fahy seems here to overlook the fact the Crawford and Rossiter do give a real place to faith development in the Religion classroom – albeit an *indirect* one, as we shall see later on.

(2) Reflections deriving from the meaning of teaching:[22]
Apart from reflecting on religion or faith, another way of trying to discover the specific contribution that Religion teaching in schools can make to the religious development of young people is to reflect on different kinds of teaching. The best place to begin any reflection on teaching is *not* to think about schools at all, but to think about first learning to ride a bike, or to swim, or to make a salad, or to make the sign of the cross. The teacher in these situations was probably a parent or a friend.[23]

Most people are teachers at some stage in their life: occasional teachers, amateurs, rather than professionals, but *real* teachers nonetheless. They show somebody how to do something. There is a simple trust between them, a kind of basic human community, even though the context is often one-to-one. The teacher uses gestures and words. The words interpret the gestures and the learner's action-responses determine the next words from the teacher. There is a trial-and-error phase, as well as words of encouragement or correction. Eventually one learns how to do something. One has been taught.

This kind of teaching is a basic human experience and is available to everybody. In this sense, everybody has a teaching charism, e.g. a parent teaching a child to pray, a parish team teaching a child how to worship, a granny teaching a young person respect for the elderly, a friend showing children and adults how to blow big bubbles. Some people are better at it than others. This kind of *ordinary* teaching does not involve academic work, textbooks, study or writing. It flows from the quality of the personal relationships involved, and the sharing of time together. It is based on modelling behaviour, sharing words (W), correcting gestures (G) and affirming effort. Tone of voice can be crucial, just as when teaching animals. This ordinary teaching could be called *'immediate teaching'*, in the sense that a very close relationship exists between teacher and pupil $(T < \frac{W}{G} > P)$. And that is why it might also be called *family teaching* or *community teaching*. It's what is meant by the phrase, 'parents are the primary educators or teachers of their children'.

Where does school teaching fit in to all this? Obviously, many aspects of school teaching are similar to what happens in *ordinary/immediate teaching*. But there are differences as well, and these differences make school teaching *extraordinary*. The school teacher is a professional, the location is a special one, the curriculum is laid down, there are books to be read, there are writing and discussion, homework and assignments, tests and assessment. The strangest aspect of school teaching is that most of the words used by school teachers refer directly not to gestures but to other words $(T < \frac{W}{(W)} > P)$. The relationship between the school teacher and pupils is mediated through these 'other words' (e.g. the words of a poem or a psalm or a parable, the mathematical symbols, the map, or the chemistry formula). School teaching can rightly be termed a '*mediate*' form of teaching. The main, though not the only, focus of all school teaching is on these 'other words' (Ws) and, therefore, on intellectual knowledge, the education of the emotions and the learning of thinking skills. This is the meaning conveyed by Moran in the following aphorism: 'academic criticism should be the centrepiece of classroom instruction'.[24]

Since schools are a part of life, and expressions of human community, they are also places where *ordinary teaching* inevitably takes place. But this happens whether or not schools want it to happen. And its range of application can easily be confined by the nature of school as an institution. Though schools are encouraged to practise some forms of *community/family teaching*,[25] this ordinary teaching is not the reason for the setting up of schools in the first place. The school, precisely as school, is designed to specialise in school teaching. Clearly we are talking here about different forms of teaching that happen in different contexts. The distinctiveness and also the relatedness of these different educational forms is well captured in these words of Moran:

> ...the school can convey **knowledge** only in the context where the school is a kind of a **community**, where school is experienced as real **work** and where a sense of retirement or **retreat** is also present.[26]

There are two extremes to be avoided here. One is the *overestimation* of the power of school teaching. It is unlikely that even the very best school teaching of Religion will ever bring about increased Mass attendance among rebellious teenagers or make dishonest pupils honest overnight. Such areas of life are more likely to be influenced by factors outside the school, such as home background, peer-group pressure, experience of local parish, etc. School teaching of Religion cannot be expected to bring about religious conversion, so it should not be faulted for failing to do what it is manifestly not able to do. Religion teaching in school has real and important aims, but they are quite limited. Religion teaching aims at knowledge, not maturity.[27] Of course, the former may eventually lead to the latter. But equally, it may not.

The other extreme to be avoided in Religion classrooms is the *neglecting* of school teaching and its replacement by too much *ordinary/immediate teaching*. This latter form is more likely to be effective on retreats outside the school, where personal sharing and discussion of experience is more appropriate, where revealing oneself and one's commitments is not felt as a threat to one's privacy. School teaching of Religion through reading, writing, analysing and discussing content ought not to be neglected. This is how the Religion class in school can become a 'privileged place' for facing the challenges posed by culture to faith.[28]

How can one imagine RE as an academic subject?
There are many factors that can minimise the status of the subject Religion in schools today. When Religion doesn't count for the Leaving Certificate; when it is not taught and assessed in as challenging and as rigorous a way as other subjects; when it has no perceived value for future employment; or when Religion class periods are taken over by other subjects, in any of these circumstances Religion teaching can seem to be without any real worth. Now that Religious Education is a State examination subject, its status may improve. But this will not happen automatically. Status will be high only if classes are well conducted, if good work is done, and if the course is diligently studied.[29] Examinations, *per se*, may achieve little of real worth.

Some problems can arise at present when Religion is not yet an examination subject, and pupils are not used to bringing work material such as pens or books in to class. Resentment is natural at being asked to work. This does not mean that work in Religion class will always be undervalued. Pupils' dissatisfaction with Religion class may be less a sign of their lack of interest in Religion and more a sign of teaching that does not challenge them, or teaching that compromises their freedom.

Another set of problems can arise if Religion is treated as a non-subject (what is often called a 'doss class'). In this case, there will be an inevitable tendency to have less class periods. This, in turn, can lead to a status problem. When Religion is not ever examined in school, informal classes will often be preferred to a more formal approach. But, if too much informality occurs, then Religion can easily be perceived as a waste of time. When there is no terminal examination to help focus on obligatory material, teachers can easily be tempted to conduct many discussions of those topics that are of immediate interest to pupils. However, this tendency to pander to pupils' wishes can create a cosy and unchallenging environment, wherein pupils will never ask for more work. A major outcome of all this is often the compromising of the professional skills of the teacher. An even worse outcome, according to one Irish Religion teacher, is the danger of offering the class something unworthy of them as human beings:

> I had underestimated him, and his fellow pupils. I also felt that in my own teaching I had given the class something which was unworthy of their questions, unworthy of their dignity, and, in fact, of their intelligence. I felt I had trivialised, and indeed tranquillised, the urge towards transcendence which was now clearly in evidence among them, and which I think is latent in everybody.[30]

It is unfortunate if Religion teachers should forget that the teenage years is the time when 'budding intellectualism is flourishing'.[31]

People also claim that there are problems when Religion is treated as a subject like all others. If it becomes an academic subject, perhaps its **uniqueness** will be compromised, perhaps its **personal** value will be lost. This worry has been well expressed over many years by Religion teachers in Ireland. In a published report of a major national survey, a substantial number of respondents claimed that a senior cycle RE examination 'would destroy the faith dimension of RE'.[32]

Modern idiom assumes that the word 'academic' means insignificant, irrelevant, meaningless or pointless. To that perception I say: 'academic' Religion does *not* have to mean irrelevant or too abstract, or too oriented to prospective third-level pupils, or too exam-dominated. It *can* mean (a) a department of Religion teachers, (b) teaching with the same skill, intellectual challenge and rigour as other subjects, (c) what is potentially the most educationally valuable subject in the curriculum (this is so, I claim, *because* Religion touches people at every level of their being: aesthetic, creative, critical, cultural, emotional, intellectual, moral, bodily, political, social and spiritual).[33]

Intellectual study of this academic kind is quite compatible with lively personal discussion. Good personal discussions often flow quite naturally from well-run Religion classes, where plenty of content is considered. The experience I have had over many years of seminar work with fourth-year Mater Dei student teachers, in connection with texts already read and studied by them, confirms for me this basic insight. Here is another example of something mentioned earlier. Teaching, like life, achieves many results that were never directly aimed at. It is common human experience that, when people set their hearts on securing their own personal happiness, it often eludes them. Paradoxically, when people aim at helping other people, they often find (to their surprise) that they have found a measure of personal happiness.

To overcome some of the problems associated with Religion as an academic subject, the school authorities would need to ensure that:

- Retreats, liturgy and prayer would still be freely available for all pupils. School would continue to socialise young people into Catholic religious practice, although older pupils would not be expected automatically to take part in prayer and liturgy. An aesthetically pleasing prayer room or chapel might well be provided.
- The responsibility for pastoral care would still rest on the entire school staff.
- Religion, as well as being taught, would continue to have a prominent place in the life of the school. Voluntary religious groups would continue to be developed, e.g. St Vincent de Paul Society, prayer groups, and Bible-study groups. Here those pupils who so desired could live at some depth the religion they are also studying at some depth.

What about faith development in the classroom?[34]

The academic study of Religion in class can be *both* intellectually challenging and personally enriching. The widely used and popular 'shared Christian praxis' approach claims to be 'both academically rigorous and personally engaging, both informative and formative...[and] eminently appropriate for Irish religious education.'[35] I believe that classroom Religion teaching, while being both informative and formative, is primarily an educational exploration of religion and not *primarily* a religious experience. The Religion classroom does its best for young people's faith when it offers them a challenging education. The most appropriate way to foster the development of the religious faith of pupils in the classroom is to take the emphasis off explicit faith-sharing and to develop the educational aspects of the study of Religion. To move from a direct to an *indirect* approach is the best way, in class, to give an important place to faith. By focusing directly on the intellectual side of religion, the personal/faith side may be indirectly nourished.

It could be said about my argument so far, in favour of the *indirect* sponsorship of faith through Religion teaching, that it is too theoretical. To that criticism I reply simply that I know of at least one practical example of its implementation. If it can happen once, it can happen again. Here is an account of this *indirect* approach to faith development – an Australian experiment called 'An Open, Inquiring Study of Religion'.[36] This was a 'Religion Studies' course for final year pupils in an Australian Catholic second-level school. It was a five-period-a-week alternative to the more academically oriented Higher School Certificate programme (the equivalent of Honours Leaving Certificate or A-Level course). In other words, the pupils who took this course were not aiming at university. The Religion teacher also had the same class for the regular Catholic RE periods, which were taken by all the final-year pupils.

In exactly the same way as the new syllabuses for Religious Education have had to justify themselves educationally, the Australian 'Religion Studies' course had to justify itself on educational grounds and not on the grounds of handing on the Catholic faith tradition. So its aims were (a) to acquire knowledge, understanding and a sympathetic appreciation of world religions, including Christianity, and (b) to develop skills for studying Religion objectively and impartially.

'Religion Studies' in practice

Pupils took both examination Religion and non-examination Religion. Their reaction to the double dose of Religion was originally negative. However, they changed their minds with time once they experienced the excitement of taking part in an open-ended, enquiring study of Religion, which did not presume or require explicit faith commitment. There was a further advantage in beginning with unfamiliar religions because, in this way, the pupils learned skills for studying Religion impartially without the normal prejudices associated with a study of one's own religious tradition. The strong negative stereotypes and anti-institutional feelings did not often arise.

Above all, pupils experienced a noteworthy freedom of enquiry. They enjoyed a free, critical encounter with religion as a significant part of human culture. They preferred these classes, which were for the honest, appreciative *studying* of other religions, much more than the other Religion classes, which were seen to be for the *getting* of their own religion. They saw 'Religion Studies' as providing them with the same freedom of enquiry as they experienced in English literature class, whenever religious topics or moral issues came up the re. Their thinking, as well as their knowledge, was regularly extended by having to get into the shoes of believers from other religious traditions. Being challenged, but not unduly crowded, slowly helped them to look more sympathetically at their own religion. They became more appreciative of its strengths and weaknesses. The course of study even convinced the pupils that they ought to have more knowledge of their own religious traditions.

Pupils were not required to state their own personal convictions. The teacher in class was not looking for responses that might indicate a deepening of religious faith. The classwork was not, in this sense, 'devotional'. The irony of the situation is that, *because* the teacher did not expect faith responses, this created in the pupils the very freedom they needed to be able to discuss their ideas comfortably at a personal level. What seems to be at issue here is not the presence of a personal tone in Religion class, but *how* the teacher tries to generate that personal tone. Personal discussion was generated in these Religion periods as a by-product of a study that concentrated on exploring content. This discussion allowed the pupils to 'rehearse imaginatively' a whole range of value positions, without their comments being regarded as a taking of any specific position (what I have referred to earlier as a 'stance'). It was this tactic of putting personal faith and commitment 'at some distance' from the classroom (putting them 'on the back burner', as it were) that actually created the freedom of enquiry. This difficult tactic provided the proper respect, space and freedom that pupils' faith deserved.

At the fair-ground, people often ride the horses on a carousel. When they are on the horses, they are at the heart of the matter, immersed in the action; educationally, this is like catechesis or denominational religious instruction. When they are off the horses but still standing beside the horses on the spinning platform, they are at a limited distance from the centre, and this is like the kind of 'Religion Studies' being discussed here. The other possibility is to be off the platform altogether and to be looking in from the outside, totally removed from the action. This is, perhaps, the kind of Religious Studies that some people find inadequate.

The 'Religion Studies' course undertaken in Australia was a respectful study of a whole range of different religions. The participants learned *about* religion in general (the great world religions); they also learned to reflect *within* religion (their own); and, later on, were sufficiently skilled to be able to learn *from* any or all of these religions. In other words, as soon as the pupils began to ask what this material meant for them personally, a more critical and evaluative study of Religion flowed naturally from the original respectful study.

In addition, the pupils acquired a sound historical perspective, as well as a confidence in their own ability to enquire critically, rationally and responsibly into religious issues. These were great safeguards against religious fundamentalism and religious naivety. The outcome was the development of responsible, rational, critical believers.[37] One notes a very similar perspective in the new Junior Certificate syllabus, which provides a comprehensive 'educational rationale' for RE in the curriculum: 'Religious Education should ensure that students are exposed to a broad range of religious traditions and to the non-religious interpretation of life. It has a particular role to play in the curriculum in the promotion of tolerance and mutual understanding. It seeks to develop in students the skills needed to engage in meaningful dialogue with those of other, or of no, religious traditions' (p. 4). In the forthcoming Leaving Certificate syllabus, Section C (*World Religions*), under the heading of attitude objectives, one finds the following: 'tolerance of and respect for the religious beliefs of other individuals and other cultures; critical discernment when encountering new religious movements.'

Conclusion

On the basis of the arguments put forward in this chapter, I am convinced that given well-prepared teachers and well-motivated pupils, the new RE syllabuses can *indirectly* assist the development of pupils' faith. However, not every school will offer examination RE; not every pupil will opt to study it. Maybe this is a good thing. I mentioned earlier that it is not an easy manoeuvre to put faith on the back burner. In pleading that teachers be brave enough to attempt this process in Religion class, I am voicing the hope of many who welcome the advent of examination Religion in our schools. But this voice is not the only valid one in our educational conversation. For an alternative voice, warning against erecting too great a barrier between a committed stance and a rational critique, and warning, too, about expecting *all* believers to be capable of such a critical attitude, hear what Lloyd and Astley have to say.[38]

Notes

1. See *RDECS*, pars. 24-39. See also K. Williams, 'Religious Ethos and State Schools', *Doctrine and Life* (November 1992), pp. 561-570; and J. Arthur, 'The Catholic School and its Curriculum', *BJRE* 14 (3), 1992, pp. 157-168.

2. See J. M. Feheney, 'Pastoral Care in a Catholic School Today', in J. M. Feheney (ed.), *From Ideal to Action*, pp. 85-100 and *Beyond the Race for Points: Aspects of Pastoral Care in a Catholic School Today*.

3. See J. Crilly, 'A National Curriculum for some: What about the others?' in St Mary's CBGS, *Ethos and Education*, no. 3 (Belfast: Summer 1997).

4. For a fine analysis of the important work of school chaplains, see L. Monahan and C. Renehan, *The Chaplain: A Faith Presence in the School Community* (Dublin: Columba, 1998).

5. See L. S. McCarthy, *Creating Space for RE. The Ballygall Project: Theory and Practice*.

6. An interview on the RTÉ *Arts Programme*, 10 October 1995. Thomas Groome makes a similar point when he argues that all forms of education can foster 'a spirituality for everyone' (*EFL*, p. 332; that 'a life-giving spirituality should permeate all education' (*EFL*, p. 345).

7. Many of the ideas and insights in this chapter come from the Australian religious educators M. Crawford and G. Rossiter, and are summarised in their book *MTC*, p. 66.

8. See A. Looney, 'Teaching Religion to Young People Today', in J. M. Feheney (ed.), *From Ideal to Action*, pp. 80-81.

9. According to the Catholic Bishops' Conference of England and Wales, *Statement on Religious Education in Catholic Schools*, 'classroom religious education will be a challenging educational engagement between the pupil, the teacher and the authentic subject material.' (p. 7)

10. W. Meijer, 'The Non-Identity of Religious Education and Religion', *BJRE* 9 (2), 1987, p. 100.

11. S. Sutherland, 'Concluding Remarks', in M. C. Felderhof (ed.), *Religious Education in a Pluralist Society*, p. 140.

12. The work of Fowler is based on this assumption of faith as 'a

universal human concern'. See J. W. Fowler, *Stages of Faith: The Psychology of Human Development and the Quest for Meaning*, p. 5.

13. See G. Moran, 'Of a Kind and To a Degree', in M. Mayr (ed.), *Does the Church Really Want Religious Education?*, p. 22. See also J. Boyers, *Religious Meaning-Making, passim.*

14. T. Sallnow, 'Catechesis or Religious Education?', in D. O'Leary (ed.), *REYA*, p. 28.

15. See A. P. Purnell, *Our Faith Story*, p. 74. Similar points are made by D. Piveteau, 'School, Society and Catechetics', in D. Lane (ed.), *Religious Education and the Future*, pp. 21-22, which talks about schooling in terms of 'knowledge and know-how'; and also by M. Warren, 'The Catechumen in the Kitchen' (*op. cit.*), p. 83, in his reference to 'religious literacy'. See also, W. D. Robinson, 'The Skills of Thinking and the RE Teacher', *BJRE* 10(2), 1988, pp. 79-85; M. Leahy, 'Indoctrination, Evangelization, Catechesis and Religious Education', *BJRE* 12 (3), 1990, pp. 137-144; The New Zealand syllabus: UF, p. 12; B. Watson, *The Effective Teaching of RE*, pp. 1-11; and J. Hull, 'Religion and Education in a Pluralist Society', in D. Lane (ed.), *Religion, Education and the Constitution*, pp. 16-33.

16. See Sacred Congregation for Catholic Education, *The Catholic School*, pars. 3, 29.

17. An idea similar to this can be found in Catholic Bishops' Conference of England and Wales, *Religious Education: Curriculum Directory for Catholic Schools*, which talks of 'religiously literate young people' (p. 10).

18. See Sacred Congregation for Catholic Education, *Lay Catholics in Schools*, par. 28.

19. T. Groome, 'A Future for Christian Religious Education,' *DL* (July/August 1992), p. 375.

20. See M. Crawford and G. Rossiter, *MTC*, p. 58.

21. P. S. Fahy, *Faith in Catholic Classrooms*, p. 117.

22. For a stimulating reflection on teaching, considered 'religiously and imaginatively rather than technically or psychologically', see M. Harris, *Teaching and Religious Imagination*, p. xiv.

23. See G. Moran, *Religious Education as a Second Language*, pp. 64-69.

24. G. Moran, *Showing How: The Act of Teaching*, p. 138.
25. See Sacred Congregation for Catholic Education, *CS*, par. 32.
26. See G. Moran, *REASL*, p. 43. (I have highlighted the key words, each of which, for Moran, is a specific educational value linked to the four fundamental educational forms, viz. schooling, family, job and leisure.)
27. This point is forcefully made in *RDECS*, par. 69, and also in *LCS*, par. 56.
28. *RDECS*, par. 52.
29. See the discussion of the advantages and the drawbacks of offering Religion for examination at Leaving Certificate level, in the Catechetical Association of Ireland *Newsletter*, Vol. 5, no. 3, 1992. See also B. Watson, 'Can RE be Assessed?', *ETRE*, pp. 142-157; K. Williams, 'Public Examinations and RE', *The Furrow* (July/August 1995), pp. 437-441; and M. Convey, 'Public Examinations and Religious Education', *The Furrow* (Nov. 1995), pp. 634-639 and comments by D. Johnson and K. Williams, *ibid.*, pp. 655-659. See also E. Ó hÉideáin, 'Religious Instruction in Schools', *DL* (May/June 1995), pp. 353-361.
30. A. Walsh, *FRIE*, p. 65.
31. V. B. Gillespie, *The Experience of Faith*, p. 53.
32. J. A. Weafer and A. Hanley, *Whither Religious Education?*, p. 86. M. A. Convey, *Keeping the Faith in a Changing Society* seems to echo this sentiment (pp. 32-34).
33. See P. M. Devitt, 'Religious Education as an Examination Subject: Identifying some newly emerging questions', in *REA* (2000), where I develop this theme. For a statement of the educational and religious values of RE, see M. Grimmitt, 'The Use of Religious Phenomena in Schools', *BJRE* 13 (2), 1991, pp. 77-88.
34. For a good overview and evaluation of faith development theory in relation to Religious Education, see M. Harris, 'Completion and Religious Education', and C. Dykstra, 'Faith Development and Religious Education', in C. Dykstra and S. Parks (eds.), *Faith Development and Fowler*.
35. T. Groome, *op. cit.*, p. 376. See also F. Hurl, 'Catechetics or Academics?' in *The Furrow* (May 2000), who argues that Religious Education should be 'both catechetical and academic' (p. 284).

36. See M. Crawford and G. Rossiter, *TRSS*, pp. 45-52; G. Rossiter, 'A Cognitive Basis for Affective Learning in Classroom RE', *BJRE* 11(1), 1988, pp. 4-10; and especially M. Crawford and G. Rossiter, 'The Secular Spirituality of Youth: Implications for Religious Education', *BJRE* 18 (3), 1996, pp. 133-143.

37. See *TRSS*, p. 51. See also J. M. Hull, 'Christian Nurture and Critical Openness', in L. Francis and A. Thatcher (eds.), *CPFE*, pp. 306-319; and L. Francis and A. Thatcher (eds.), *Studies in Religion and Education*, Chapter 17, 'Christian Faith and the Open Approach to Religious Education'.

38. I. Lloyd, 'Confession and Reason', *BJRE* 8 (3), 1986, pp. 140-145; and J. Astley, *PCRE*, p. 103.

Chapter 4

HOW TO TEACH PRAYER?

Strictly speaking, catechesis and religious instruction are not the same. Though closely related, they beat with a different pulse. There are many ways of describing the difference, e.g. *RDECS* states that catechesis aims at maturity of faith, while religious instruction aims at knowledge and understanding of the faith. This issue of two closely related, but distinct activities, was a major theme in Chapter 3 when I was exploring the main purpose of the Religion class. I pointed out there that, together with all the school staff, the Religion teacher shares in the catechetical mission of the school, but that, over and above this, the Religion teacher also makes a specific contribution to pupils' faith development within the Religion classroom. Here is where the Religion teacher offers pupils what is not readily available in other contexts, namely, a challenging educational encounter with religion. For those who truly believe, this encounter can both deepen knowledge (a *direct* aim) and help faith to mature (an *indirect* aim). If there are pupils who do not believe, or whose faith is not Christian, such a challenging educational encounter with religion will have mainly a knowledge outcome.

From the point of view of the Religion teacher, the teaching in the same room can have a different tone at different times. On one occasion, it can have an educational or 'explaining' tone. At another time, it might have a 'showing how' or catechetical tone. When teaching in an 'explaining' mode, the Religion teacher examines a particular religious topic in these terms: 'this is what *people* do/believe/hope in; here are the reasons why *people* do/believe/hope; you yourself may or may not want to try this out for yourself'. In this 'explaining' mode, the teacher invites the pupils to stand back from religion to a certain extent, so that they can gain a bird's-eye view of it. This is not at all an easy manoeuvre.

In the 'showing how' mode, the Religion teacher explores the same religious topic in this manner: 'this is how *we* do it; here are the reasons why *we* do it; try it out for yourself and discover for yourself the truth of what I am saying'. Here the approach is like that of a meeting-facilitator or a sports-coach. The assumption is that everybody shares the same faith experience, but that one of the group is better able to interpret for the others what they are all going through. The difference between the 'explaining' (or educational or 'bird's-eye') mode, on the one hand, and the 'showing how' (or catechetical or 'facilitational/coaching') mode, on the other, is captured by the use of two different key words. The 'explainer' looks at *'people'* in general; the 'facilitator/coach' is a member of the *'we'* in question. In other words, the explainer/educator adopts a more intellectual (or objective) approach; while the catechist/facilitator/coach uses a more relational (or inter-subjective) approach.

The title of this chapter, 'How to teach prayer?' can have two distinct meanings: 'how to explain prayer?' (educational tone), or 'how to show pupils how to pray?' (catechetical tone). I assume that Religion teachers will know which mode to adopt and when. For the sake of argument, however, I shall now concentrate on the following imaginary situation: *'I am a Religion teacher, employed as a catechist to teach in a school with mainly Catholic pupils. I have often been asked to organise prayer sessions and liturgies with my pupils. I have also tried to explain to them the meaning and purpose of Christian prayer, as well as the difficulties involved in it.*[1] *I wonder will I be able to teach the Junior Certificate syllabus Section on "The Celebration of Faith" or the Leaving Certificate syllabus Section on "Worship, Prayer and Ritual." What benefits, if any, will accrue to the pupils from my teaching of this material? I am committed to eight principles of teaching prayer. Can I remain faithful to these prayer principles while teaching the new syllabuses?'* In the text that now follows, two voices will speak in turn. Firstly, the voice of catechesis. This will be in italics. Then will come, in Roman script, the voice of religious education. The first voice is primarily concerned with 'teaching the Way'; the second with 'teaching to understand Religion.'[2]

The principle of experience

I believe that it is better for pupils to be praying than just hearing teachers talk about prayer. As a catechist, I have to talk a lot about prayer as I explain why people need prayer, as I outline the many approaches to prayer, the richness of the Christian tradition of prayer, etc. However, this in itself will never be sufficient if my pupils are to become genuine 'pray-ers'. It is essential that pupils actually have some genuine experiences of prayer. To enable pupils actually to take part in different forms of prayer at different times during the year is a major factor in expanding their religious experience. On this basis it should then be easier for me to deepen their understanding of prayer. This is an example of the principle that people learn by doing. One learns the meaning of prayer by actually praying. My teaching role here is to make possible this praying, either within the classroom (on occasion) or within the school (if there be a prayer-room).

In articulating this principle, you are clearly in a 'showing how' mode; you are trying directly to foster faith commitment in your pupils through leading them into a deeper prayer life. To that extent you are clearly going *beyond* the direct purpose of the new syllabuses, which state that students' 'personal faith commitment and/or affiliation to a particular religious grouping will not be subject to assessment for national certification'.[3] Whenever you are teaching prayer through the new syllabuses, therefore, you can afford to relax and allow the entire school community (which also includes you) to foster your pupils' prayer life. While focusing on the new syllabuses, you are entitled to occasionally doff your catechetical cap and don your educational cap. For example, you may encourage your pupils to observe an experience of worship, not primarily for worship's sake, but so that they can 'see the elements of worship in action' (p. 34: a learning outcome). But note too that, even when you revert to your formal catechetical mode, you cannot avoid talking and explaining. These teaching skills, developed by you in the educational mode, are also central to good practice in a strictly catechetical mode and are readily transferable to it.

The double principle of motivation and format

I always try to remember that Jesus was a man of prayer. One might spend a whole year trying to give pupils reasons why they ought to pray. Instead, one might simply point to Jesus and the hectic life he lived. He prayed – obviously because he needed to pray.[4] And he allowed his example to spark off a kind of wonderment among his disciples. It was this wonderment that led them to ask him to teach them to pray. And when he replied, he invited them to pray as he was accustomed to pray – to learn of him, to follow his example, to use the structure or format he himself used: 'Let your prayer be addressed to your common Father. Let it be a prayer of praise; let it be a prayer that the Father's kingdom may come among you and among all human beings. Let is also be a prayer of petition for your daily needs, a prayer made on the express condition that the Father's will be done and not your own will. Let your prayer ask especially for forgiveness from God upon all people so that you will in turn be graced into an ability to forgive others. Let your prayer ask God's saving presence to enliven you as you struggle through the challenges, the crises and the temptations of life.'

The Lord's prayer [5] is probably as close as we can ever get to the basic format or structure of the prayer-life of Jesus. It is true, of course, that we have had to modify the format somewhat, so that we can pray for forgiveness of our own personal sins. Nevertheless, the fact remains that Jesus has given us an example of how to pray. We 'learn of him' not only when we learn the format of his prayer, but also when we learn that, like him, we too need always to pray.

In any approach to teaching prayer, either catechetical or educational, it is clearly acceptable to direct pupils' attention to Jesus as a man of prayer, and as a teacher of prayer. The new syllabuses try to go even further than this. At Junior Certificate level, pupils learning the meaning of prayer are invited to look at 'important people in the spiritual traditions' (p. 37). Pupils are also told the 'stories of faithful people from two religious traditions' so that they can understand 'prayer and worship as expressions of religious faith and search for God' (p. 30). This opening up of broader perspectives on prayer is continued at Leaving Certificate level, where the proposed new syllabus deliberately introduces pupils to a great many practitioners of prayer. Section G, 3.1 presents Buddha and Ignatius as teachers of meditation. Section G, 3.3 examines the mystic tradition, mainly though not entirely within Christianity. It presents John of the Cross, Teresa of Avila, Siddhartha Gautama, Julian of Norwich, Thomas à Kempis and Catherine of Siena.[6] Section G, 2.4c explores prayer forms from religious traditions other than Christianity.

Jesus may be the rose in God's garden, but he would surely want his followers to treasure the daisies and violets and buttercups too. To study prayer as a facet of *all* religious experience is important for Christians, because it alerts them to the wider world of religion and to its place in God's plan. The sight of Muslims at prayer could be a powerful lesson for believing Catholics. This will be a major theme in Chapter 8, *Why Teach World Religions?*

The principle of variety

A good teacher knows many ways to pray.[7] When praying the official prayers of the Church, especially the psalms, one is constantly impressed by the great variety of sentiments that find expression in these prayers. Whenever one turns to the popular prayers of the Church (the litanies, novenas, rosaries, prayer groups, Taizé prayer, etc.), one is very conscious once again of the rich diversity both of format and technique of prayer. It is obvious that no teacher will be inclined or even able to arrange for every kind of prayer-experience in school. However, the principle still holds true that variety is the spice of life. Such variety can give flavour to the prayer-life of young maturing believers.[8]

It is rather sad to realise that many young Christians today feel obliged to search outside the Christian tradition for a prayer-life they feel is not afforded them within the normal structures of the faith. The tragedy is that there is a very rich Christian prayer tradition, the variety of which has much to offer them, but that often teachers are either insufficiently aware of it or unable or unwilling to share in this richness with their pupils.[9] I recall with pleasure that one American catechist produced a very helpful book which should be of great assistance to teachers.[10]

In this context, too, one should mention a growing tendency of certain teachers 'to pray out of life' before their class from time to time. They pray in response to events, as reported in the daily papers, and then encourage members of the class to do the same. This practice can introduce not just variety but a vitality of expression into the experience of prayer, and can ultimately lead to a richness in the liturgical bidding prayers, which is often noticeably lacking.[11]

You are clearly in a catechetical mode here again. But notice one point you made, about teachers being insufficiently aware of the variety of prayer forms in the Christian tradition. If that is so, then a careful study of the Junior Certificate syllabus Section E5 on 'Prayer' will alert you to various forms of prayer such as 'meditation, contemplation, petition, praise and thanksgiving, penitence, etc.' (p. 37). When the Leaving Certificate syllabus comes on stream, Section G will give you 'examples of traditional prayers of the Christian tradition' (2.4a), 'Ignatian meditation' (3.1g), 'some contemplative traditions' (3.2a), and 'characteristics of the mystical traditions' (3.3b). That pupils become more aware of this great variety could be a key objective in your teaching.

The principle of freedom

You cannot force prayer on people. Prayer that is not freely undertaken is less than real prayer. Christ has set us free in the hope that we might use this freedom to commit ourselves through him to Our Father, in the power of the Holy Spirit. Since the ideal Christian commitment is one that is freely assumed, it follows that the ideal Christian prayer-life is one that is freely desired and entered into. Teachers and managers need to take this principle seriously into account when trying to ensure that praying is a real part of school life. This must happen within the context of the basic freedom of all people concerned.

No two schools will achieve a similar balance between the values of prayer and freedom, but some balance must be found, in the name of genuine Christian education. Freedom means the right to weigh and choose values.[12] What I have already said about generating experiences of prayer, about strong motivation for prayer in the prayer-life of Jesus, about the basic format of all Christian prayer, and about the importance of having a variety of prayer experiences, is the raw material for freedom in prayer. You are not really free to pray if you haven't experienced some real prayer, if you don't know why you pray, if you don't know the shape of it, or if you have no idea of the range of options in prayer that are open to you.

You are perfectly right to state that *freedom* is fundamental to Christian living, and so should be fostered within every catechetical activity. Freedom is also fundamental to the educational process, and so should be cultivated within every Religion class. In fact, the new syllabuses regard freedom as being so educationally important that Junior Certificate pupils are explicitly introduced to the notion of freedom (p. 39). As a further development of this central theme, Leaving Certificate Section D, 4.1d (*Moral Decision-Making*) formally examines 'the issue of freedom'. It is clear, therefore, that catechesis and religious education share a common commitment to the advancement of pupils' freedom. However, there is a difference between catechetical freedom and classroom freedom.

In strict catechesis, a free choice of Catholic faith is assumed to have already been made by every participant. The marks of a valid catechesis are that it is both limited by and enriched by 'freedom within' this commitment. On the other hand, the Religion classroom in which the new syllabuses are studied cannot *assume* such prior acceptance of and commitment to the Catholic faith. At every moment of the educational encounter with Religion, pupils (including Catholics) must be free to stand back from any particular religious or non-religious commitment that already shapes their lives. In short, the new syllabuses of Religious Education must be capable of being taken by *any* pupil in *any* class in *any* school in Ireland, irrespective of the denominational character or the level of intensity of the pupil's religious commitment, or indeed of the very presence or absence of any specific religious commitment.

In the catechetical meaning of freedom, one important aspect is knowledge of the range of prayer options available to the believer. Such knowledge may foster a growing freedom in one's prayer life. Insofar as the new syllabuses provide an introduction to a relatively wide range of prayer styles, one might claim that they thereby *indirectly* offer some modest assistance to the catechetical ministry of the classroom.

The principle of shared values

It is my firm conviction that, if you don't pray, you can't teach others to pray.[13] This follows because the Christian faith is basically a way of discipleship. It is a way of life, and much more than a set of ideas. One learns a way of life (as distinct from a set of ideas) only by a gradual assimilation both of practices and of the values underlying these practices. There is a sense in which one needs a guru who incarnates these values and allows them to be caught, as it were, by others. That is why nobody can ever really teach others to pray unless regular prayer is part of their own experience. 'Out of the abundance of the heart, the mouth speaks'.

There is a similarity here to the case of the teacher of literature. In order to teach literature well, one must be an avid reader of literature. One must at least like poetry, or even be a poet oneself, in order to teach poetry effectively. That is why one must have a genuine feel for prayer, for its values in one's life, and for the strange problems it poses, if one is ever to communicate an enthusiasm for and love of prayer that can survive the stresses and ambiguities of everyday life.

Once again you are talking in a catechetical mode, about 'showing how' to pray, about coaching believers in the art of praying as Catholics, about pointing out how well they are doing, and indicating how they might try to do things differently. This can never be the *explicit* focus of the new syllabuses, which aim at knowledge and understanding of prayer rather than practice of a prayer-life, and so must, by definition, avoid any terminal assessment of pupils' 'personal faith commitment' (for commitment, here, read prayer-life).

However, if while teaching the new syllabuses, you adopt the 'explaining' mode of teaching prayer, this can have some interesting *indirect* catechetical impact on some of your pupils. If you explain the format and frequency of Muslim prayer to sceptical young Catholics, this *might* give them a new motivation to enter more fully into their own neglected Catholic prayer. If you explain why some Catholics find the Rosary so powerful a prayer, then, even if you do not experience its value in your own life, you *might* indirectly introduce some young Catholics into its mysteries.

The 'principle of shared values' works slightly differently in catechesis and in religious education. In catechesis, 'shared values' is like a player/manager coaching young footballers in the art of soccer (because they all share a love for soccer). In religious education, 'shared values' is like an *aficionado* of running inviting young people to take up hurling (because they all share a love of sport).

The principle of interiority

One should never confuse 'saying prayers' with 'praying prayers'.[14] As children, we learn to 'say our prayers'. The two main functions of learning set prayers are, firstly, to enable us to join with others in public prayer and, secondly, to offer us a standard prayer language. A certain uniformity of language is clearly a value. However, one needs always to remember that interiority is more important in some ways even than the words we use in prayer. The prophets had to remind the people of Israel, on behalf of Yahweh, that 'these people honour me with their lips but their hearts are far from me'. The King in Hamlet comments that, 'My words fly up, my thoughts remain below: Words without thoughts never to heaven go' (Act 3, Sc. 3).

Interiority, the 'heart', really meaning what one says, throwing one's whole self behind the recited or sung words – this is an absolute necessity for genuine Christian prayer. One good way of seeing to it that set prayer formulas are more than a mere mouthing of words, is to encourage children even from the early years to engage in more informal and perhaps even some non-vocal kinds of prayer. As the children develop interiority in these spontaneous prayers, it may happen that this interiority will transfer itself even to their more formal recitations of prayer. In this context, one could cite the value of encouraging young people to read such books of informal prayer that best suit their mentality.[15]

Here is a catechetical principle that transcends catechesis, because it applies to the whole of life. Everything in life is better, if it is what it seems to be. Nobody likes a sham. Style without substance is dead. If the prayer-life of religious people is a fake, then it becomes easy for the unbeliever to become apathetic about religion. This catechetical 'principle of interiority' has great relevance in the Religion class, especially for those who are non-believers or even shallow believers. How else might they develop even an initial interest in a living religion?

The principle of wasting time creatively[16]

It is crucial for pupils to give God some time. Time for prayer is important, not so much to enable us to say many prayers, as to enable God to work upon our hearts and transform them into images of his Son. The time we spend in prayer could, of course, be a time when 'We besiege him with selfish petitions, we weary him with our petty ambitions'.[17] *It could indeed be a time in which we try to convert God to our way of thinking, so that God will give us what we ask for, which we think we know is best for us.*[18] *But a healthier view of prayer would see it as the time when we make ourselves available to the active power of God's transforming spirit.*

This was the thrust of Jesus' often going off to a lonely place to pray. He prayed so that his will might become more and more aligned to the will of his Father. Our basic motivation when we pray, therefore, ought to be, not that God will be changed because of what we say but, rather, that we will be changed by what God says. It is obvious that such change (or conversion) will require a lifetime. That's why we ought to pray always, even when nothing seems to happen, even when we seem to fail, for 'the attempt to pray may be as close as we can get to the real thing'. [19] *God the master craftsman has but two tools with which to sculpt us into the image of his Son – these are our freedom and our time.*

Many elements of the new syllabuses can have a relevance to this topic. For example, Honours pupils at Junior Certificate level are introduced to 'worship as response to mystery' (p. 35). In the proposed Leaving Certificate programme, in Section C, 2.1c, 'the nature of the relationship between the divine and the human' is explored in the context of at least two different religious traditions. A study of this question would probably include a consideration of the issue of 'unanswered prayers'. This question will have already been asked by Junior Certificate pupils in the treatment of 'difficulties with prayer' (p. 37).

Junior Certificate Section E, 1 ('The World of Ritual') and Leaving Certificate Sections G, 2.3a and c, all emphasise the fact that prayer needs an adequate context. Prayer needs 'sacred spaces and times'. Knowing this, a school catechist can help shape the official school policy towards prayer. If that policy provides pupils with quality time and quality space for prayer activities, then Religion teachers will be able both to foster among pupils a deeper life of prayer (catechesis) and also to explain with greater ease what lies at the very heart of prayer (religious education).

Throughout second-level schooling, pupils are expected to grow and mature in every aspect of life. At Junior Certificate level, pupils are introduced to the themes of 'growth of faith' and 'stages of faith' (p. 29). The Leaving Certificate syllabus Section D, 4.1a, explores the theme of 'growing in morality from childhood to adulthood'. While growing in morality is not precisely the same as growing in faith or growing in prayer, all these themes share a common commitment to suitable personal development. In this way, the educational world and the catechetical world share a common focus and can enrich one another.

The principle of silent listening

The essence of prayer is to open one's heart and let God in. Prayer is an expression of faith in a God who is really present to us in a personal way. Prayer is a language of faith. There should be a measure of talk in prayer. Equally there should be silent listening in prayer.[20] Prayer is dialogue rather than monologue. It is a conversation rather than a lecture. It is communication with, rather than talking at. The voice welling up from a praying heart is the voice of Samuel: 'Speak, Lord, your servant is listening'. We are not born with a ready-made ability to listen to a God who is always speaking to us in strange ways. We must learn this skill, in much the same way as we learn to listen to one another.

Hearing is easy. Listening is more demanding. It requires an openness of heart that makes us ready to accept even the annoying or uncomfortable things about ourselves. Pupils, in their growth to maturity of faith, need to be helped to learn this basic attitude. Every time they listen to one another and to the teacher in class is a foundation on which the listening attitude needed for prayer can be built. The importance of this attitude and of the silence that gives birth to it, has always been recognised in the catechetical literature.[21]

Silent listening to God in prayer cannot happen apart from a careful, attentive respect for the neighbour. In listening to God, the wholly Other, we need also to listen to all the human others. We need to be ecumenical and inclusive at heart. The explicitly ecumenical spirit of both the new syllabuses needs to be adverted to here. By ecumenical I mean open to all religious experience. Openness of this kind means being willing to continue doing what you have automatically done, as a catechist, namely, to draw ideas on Christian prayer from the world of the Jewish prophets. What the new syllabuses aspire to, however, is an even more radical ecumenism, excluding no positive religious insight from any of the great world religions.

Conclusion

This has been a long chapter, because I have tried to allow two voices to speak to one another, the catechetical and the educational. It is hard enough for these voices to appreciate one another when they belong to different people, but when they issue from a single heart, the tension can be even worse. However, I hope I have argued sufficiently well to convince even the committed catechist that these dearly held 'principles' can also be applied to the strictly educational task. And, therefore, the catechetical work can be enriched by occasionally shifting into strictly educational gear. In short, I hope I have demonstrated that teaching the Junior Certificate Sections D (*The Question of Faith*) and E (*The Celebration of Faith*), as well as the Leaving Certificate Section on *Worship, Prayer and Ritual,* can at least *indirectly* foster the worship dimension of faith.[22]

Notes

1. The following are helpful resources for Religion teachers: S. Tugwell, *Prayer*; C. Stuhlmueller, 'Prayer', in J. S. Marino (ed.), *BTRE*, pp. 169-195; John Paul II, *Catechism of the Catholic Church*, pars. 2558-2758; and D. Neary, 'Prayer in the Catechism', in P. M. Devitt (ed.), *CC*, pp. 69-77.
2. See M. Harris and G. Moran, *Reshaping Religious Education*, pp. 35, 37.
3. *Junior Certificate Religious Education Syllabus*, p. 45.
4. See J. Radermakers, 'The Prayer of Jesus in the Synoptics', in International Centre for Studies in Religious Education, *Lumen Vitae* (1969, no. 4); also T. Corbishley, *The Prayer of Jesus*.
5. See Mayhew McCrimmon, *The Sower* (Summer 1980); and also *CCC*, pars. 2759-2865.
6. For a fine examination of 'contemplation in a world of action', see C. Smith, *The Way of Paradox: Spiritual Life as taught by Meister Eckhart*.
7. See M. M. Doherty, *Dynamic Approaches to Teaching High School Religion*, Chap. 5.
8. See T. Sheaf, 'How to Pray 3: At the Kitchen Sink', *The Tablet* (9 August 1997), p. 1010.
9. For a detailed exposition of early Christian prayer forms, see D. Coggan, *The Prayers of the New Testament*. For an introduction to contemplation, see W. H. Shannon, *Seeking the Face of God*.
10. See B. Caprio, *Experiments in Prayer*.
11. A good example of vitality of expression in prayer is M. Hollings and E. Gillick, *It's me, O Lord*.
12. See B. Marthaler, *Catechetics in Context*, p. 143.
13. See J. McKenna, 'Praying with Pupils', *IrCat* (Vol. 3 no. 3).
14. See *LV* (1983, no. 3), which is devoted to 'The Time for Interior Life'.
15. Examples would be M. Quoist, *Prayers of Life;* J. Arias, *Prayer without Frills;* and D. Neary, *passim*.
16. Groome describes contemplative prayer as 'taking time to smell the roses.' See T. Groome, *EFL*, p. 152.
17. See C. R. Mitchell, 'The Soul of Jesus is Restless', in T. C. Clark, *1000 Quotable Poems*, p. 164.

18. See M. van Caster, 'The Catechesis of Petitionary Prayer', *LV* (1968, no. 2).
19. J. Devitt, 'Where Hope and History Rhyme', in D. A. Lane (ed.), *RCD*, p. 107.
20. See J. Cotter, 'How to Pray 2: Words and Silence', *The Tablet* (2 August 1997), pp. 982-3. An excellent resource for teachers who wish to give a Catholic perspective on ritual and sacramental celebration is M. Drumm and T. Gunning, *A Sacramental People.*
21. See D. Piveteau, 'Catechesis in the School Environment', *LV* (1981, no. 2).
22. For a fuller consideration of the worship dimension of faith, and a treatment of all the important actors in this drama, see P. M. Devitt, *ID*, chapter 1, 'Praying to the Father with thanks'.

Chapter 5

DARE WE HOPE?

The modern film about long-term prisoners, *The Shawshank Redemption*, constantly raises this question without ever fully answering it. For Jews and for Christians, however, the answer must be YES. The entire Bible is a story of God's faithfulness, told over and over again to sinful people, in order to encourage them and bring them hope in adversity. In the words of an eminent scholar, it is 'a counterstory about God, world, neighbour, and self ... [it] provides the materials out of which an alternatively construed world can be properly imagined'.[1] It is very fitting, therefore, that Section H of the proposed Leaving Certificate Religious Education syllabus, called *The Bible; Literature and Sacred Text*, will try to foster in pupils an 'awareness of the central place of the Bible in the Judaeo-Christian traditions' ('attitude-objective' 4c).

Of course, in their earlier journey through the Junior cycle, pupils will have already been introduced to a wide range of sacred scriptures, not only from Judaism and Christianity, but also from other great world religions such as Hinduism, Buddhism and Islam (Section C, *Foundations of Religion – Major World Religions*). Pupils at Junior Certificate level will study how these texts 'came to be in their present form'; in other words, they will learn about 'the development of the tradition from oral to written tradition'. They will also consider these 'sacred texts as documents of faith' (p. 22). Meanwhile, they will be introduced to the central Christian scriptures. After learning about the context (historical, geographical, political and religious) 'into which Jesus of Nazareth was born' (p. 15), they will then be helped to examine the 'evidence about Jesus' (p. 16). At this juncture they will trace 'the development of the Gospel from oral tradition to written word'. In doing this critical work, they will be reminded that the evangelists were 'people of faith' in Jesus the Christ, who then became proclaimers of 'good news' for all people. The pupils will read a wide variety of Gospel stories, in order to familiarise themselves with the 'different perspectives in the Gospels'.

The Junior Certificate programme will introduce pupils to the central New Testament topic, 'the kingdom of God as preached by Jesus' (p. 17). This theme will be explored in terms of the life, death and resurrection of Jesus: the means by which, for Christians, this kingdom has been introduced on earth. Pupils will study the parables and miracles of Jesus. They will examine the implications of Jesus' table-fellowship with sinners, outsiders, women and the poor. They will reflect upon Jesus' understanding of 'love of neighbour, and love of enemy'. The notion of discipleship, 'the call to follow' Jesus, will be traced from its origins in the life of Jesus to its ramifications 'in the lives of Christian believers today'. The manner in which Jesus came into 'conflict with the religious and political authorities' (p. 18), the Last Supper and death of Jesus, the appearances of the risen Jesus after his death, and 'the formation of the first Christian communities' (p. 19) – these are the dramatic beginnings of Christian history; pupils who study these episodes will learn how the Christian tradition draws its life-blood and present energy from the outpouring of Jesus' blood on Calvary, and the outpouring of the Spirit of Jesus at Pentecost. They will, perhaps, begin to recognise that the Christian story is one of hope in the face of betrayal, torture, abandonment and cruel death.

One of the key themes in the New Testament, as will be obvious from the above, is the presence of the risen Lord Jesus. I should like now to reflect and meditate at length on this theme by drawing upon selected scriptural passages and, in particular, the Johannine motif 'I am the way, the truth and the life' (Jn 14:6).[2] I hope thereby to highlight the fundamentally eschatological or hope-filled thrust of these sacred scriptures.[3]

The world has seen many great people, whom we remember with admiration. There have been great thinkers such as Plato, Aquinas, Catherine of Siena, Galileo, Einstein; great charismatic leaders such as Moses, the Buddha, Muhammad, Teresa of Avila, Gandhi, Pope John XXIII; great artists such as Hildegarde of Bingen, Shakespeare, Leonardo da Vinci, Beethoven, etc. All these people have contributed immensely to us and we today are richer because of their achievements. We owe them an enormous debt. However, since they are all dead and have gone away from us, we can only look back at them. We cannot meet them today, and this is a great drawback. What philosopher would not like to spend some time walking around with Socrates, listening to him and asking him questions? What leader would not like to feel at close quarters the charisma of Francis of Assisi? What artist would not like to be in the company of Michelangelo as he painted the roof of the Sistine Chapel?

He is risen; he is alive

There is, however, one great man who, though he died, is still alive with us today. That man is Jesus of Nazareth. In his day he was a great mind, a great leader, a great artist, a truly great person. He spoke the truth and paid the ultimate price of truth. He was killed by those who couldn't bear to hear the truth. Fortunately for us, though, and this is what our faith rests upon, his death was not the end. His Father raised him from the dead (Acts 2:24).[4] We believe that this man Jesus is now very much alive, with a new kind of life far richer than the one he lived in Palestine. The superior nature of this life is reflected in our calling him Christ or Messiah (Acts 2:36).[5] By this we mean, among other things, that he is able to bridge the span of space and time and be present to human beings in every age and in every place. His death may have separated him from his friends, but his new risen life means that he can be present to all people, and not just to a few friends. He transcends time and place and culture. His resurrection could be called an 'epidemic of life'.[6]

Jesus Christ, who is truly alive today, is present to the world in many different ways. One mode of his presence is that which applies to his 'extended body', which we refer to as the Church. This Church is like a body whose head is Jesus risen from the dead (1 Cor 6:15). All the members of the Church (those who believe in him) are like cells in his body. This body performs certain activities, which are traditionally called sacraments.[7] In each of these sacraments the whole body is active. Sacraments are well described as 'actions of the community'.[8] Jesus, the head, is active, forgiving, healing, offering himself as food, etc. The member-cells are active, accepting this forgiveness, being healed, being fed on the bread from heaven, etc.

When we say that Jesus is actively present in his Church, and actively present in the sacraments, this depends as always on one condition. The same condition as applied when he was on earth continues to apply today. Jesus can do wonders for anyone who has faith in him (Mk 5:34). Though 'Easter is primarily an event for Jesus himself… Jesus lives again through God – as a challenge to faith'.[9] In his Church, Jesus can be really alive only for those who believe in him. Believing in him means being open to his influence, and open to his Spirit. It implies letting his risen life flow through one's veins, as the life of the head flows through the rest of the body. The person we judge to have excelled in this activity of believing is none other than Mary, the woman who bore Jesus and gave him to the world as a child (Lk 1:38).[10] Christmas celebrates not just the birth of Jesus but the birth of faith that made his coming possible.

The risen Jesus invites us to share his risen life

We all recognise that there are many ways of being present to people. In a crowded bus, I am physically present to the people around me, but I may never speak to them, know them, or have anything to do with them. However, when we say that Jesus is present to people today, we don't mean this kind of presence. Rather, we refer to the way in which people who love one another are present to each other, namely, at the deepest levels of their being. Even when they are physically absent, their deep personal relationship lives and grows and deepens.

Something similar is true of the deep personal relationship that the risen Jesus sets up with all who believe in him or commit themselves to him. This relationship too can grow, deepen and mature. From his side of the relationship, we talk of the continuing gift of the life-giving Spirit (Acts 1:8). From our side of the relationship, what are involved are listening to Jesus, conversing with him, being concerned about his issues, trying to implement his wishes, trying to get to know him better and better. In other words, the faith that makes Jesus' presence an explicit reality in our Christian life must flow over into the following activities: *prayer* (listening and conversing), *moral living* (trying to implement his wishes) and *reading the Scriptures* (as a privileged way of coming to know him).[11] These are the challenges we must face in developing our relationship with Jesus, risen from the dead (Acts 2:42).

Jesus is the way

As Jesus becomes more present to us and we to him, we realise he is bringing us through life along a certain route. This route ultimately arrives back home with the Father. 'Death is a passing into God, is a homecoming into God's seclusion, is assumption into his glory'.[12] But, before death, on the way through life, the going is often tough. We feel challenged to give ourselves wholeheartedly, as Jesus did, to his Father's Kingdom, and this means giving ourselves wholeheartedly to all the other people Jesus is bringing back to the Father as well. The 'characteristics of the reign of God as preached by Jesus'[13] are peace, inclusion, and a sharing of goods. God is a God of the powerless. 'If Christ is really risen, this leads to the revolt of conscience against the hells on earth and against all those who heat them up'.[14]

The way to the Father, therefore, is a way of self-sacrifice, of concern for others, of dying to oneself in order to live for others. In a strange way, this is real freedom (1 Cor 9:19).[15] For we are freed from the tyranny and slavery of our own sinful tendencies and are set free to be of service to all people. The path we tread is a narrow path (Lk 13:24), but it leads to a new and better and freer life. Jesus himself, being raised from the dead, has in his own person already reached the Father. This same achievement is promised to all who walk his way.[16]

We can think of the risen Jesus as the first fruits (1 Cor 15:23), as the pioneer of our faith (Heb 12:2). We can also imagine him as a mighty river that has already reached the infinite sea. We, in turn, are the little tributaries and streams that, by running into him, become an integral part of him and, so, are swept along into a new and perfect life with the Father who is in heaven. This is the very basis of our *hope*. This is the meaning of the Gospel, the good news of Easter. All is not lost in death. Everything good Jesus ever did while alive on earth is preserved for ever by his Father and transformed into a new creation. And the same guarantee is ours if only we live as part of him, if only we join ourselves to him, if only we follow his way. Thus, those aspects of our day-to-day life that reflect his way of life have a guaranteed permanence. 'Anything in human life which reflects and shares the definitive human response to God will be accepted and glorified'.[17] It will survive death and come to a new and superior life. We can, in fact, bring nothing else with us through the gates of death. Anything that does not measure up to his standards is what we call sin.[18] Sin cannot survive death.

Jesus is the truth
Jesus, however, is much more than a challenge or a call to us to live in a certain way. As well as being the way, he is also the truth. When any person speaks, you know more or less who he/she is. When God speaks, we know more or less who God is. Now God speaks in many ways (Heb 1:1-2). But God has spoken and said all there is to be said about himself, in a very specific manner. In fact, the best expression available of who God really is, is not a spoken or a written word at all. It is the Word of God that is a person. It is God's flesh-word, none other than Jesus of Nazareth (Jn 1:14). Jesus is God's headline, who reveals all that is hidden in God. Jesus is God's dynamite, who explodes all human myths concerning God. When we listen to Jesus, we learn something of God's power and love and mercy. This is what divine revelation means for Christians.[19] When we look towards Jesus, we see the image or icon of the Father, and so we rightly call him Son of God (Mk 15:39).

However, when we direct our gaze towards Jesus, we see much more as well. We see what humanity is called to be. Jesus the human being is a living example of what all human beings can be. Jesus is as much the truth about human beings as he is the truth about God. As we look at him, we see one of our own kind who responded perfectly to God's appeal that people would return his great love, even unto death. God, for his part, has replied by raising this man Jesus from the dead. And now this risen Jesus is inviting us, in turn, to respond as he did to our common Father. He is inviting us to become one with him and thereby to become fully alive, to become more real people, to become more truly human, to achieve real human wholeness, integrity and success. This is our vocation – to enter into his kingdom (Mt 4:17).

Jesus is the life

This vocation is literally a matter of life and death. Jesus is the vine, we are the branches (Jn 15:5). If we join ourselves to him (by faith commitment), we live with his new life. His new risen life flows in our veins, like vine-sap through vine-branches. If ever we separate ourselves from him, we will surely wither and die, just as leaves do in the fall. We are grafted on to Jesus and begin to share his life when he pours on us his Spirit on the day of our baptism (Acts 2:38). Should we detach ourselves from him by serious sin, he is only too willing to graft us back on again. This is the reason for the sacrament of reconciliation.[20] In the last analysis, real life and real salvation are impossible for us unless we become a part of Jesus, unless we live in his Spirit. This is what we often refer to as the gracious plan of the Father.

To summarise, this *scriptural* reflection falls into five sections:

(1) Jesus is *alive*. He is risen and is actively *present* here and now.
(2) This is so that *we* may be able to share in this new life.
(3) He is the *way* to this life.
(4) He is the *truth*.
(5) He is this very *life*.

All of this is implied in our calling Jesus the Christ, or the Messiah, or the anointed one (Mk 8:29). By this we mean that he is the very core of God's plan for the human race and the entire world.[21] He is the 'synthesis' of our faith.[22] If we keep him in the foreground of our thoughts we can see how the many aspects of our faith fit in together.[23] He is truly the cornerstone, for he holds together the edifice of our faith (Eph 2:20-21).

Conclusion

I shall argue very strongly in Chapter 7 for giving more time to the teaching of Church history, because a sense of history can alert pupils to the richness and the poverty of the great Christian Tradition. In this chapter, I have placed a similar emphasis on teaching the Holy Scriptures. I have also tried to show at the same time how a careful study of the Scriptures, as part of the new syllabuses, can provide a valuable educational encounter with the Christian faith. By reflecting on Jesus Christ as the very centre of the Christian faith, I have developed a simple overview of that faith as a guarantee of *hope*. I have hinted that this hope-filled faith could well stop people being 'ruled ... by expectations, fears, anxieties and ambitions' and help them instead 'to live fully in the present and to savour the giftedness of the moment we have now'.[24] Here is a healthy vision of life that Religion teachers could profitably explore in class as they accompany their pupils' search for truth[25] and life and a living hope. In 'making religious education more imbued with the biblical perspective and more interpenetrated with biblical insights',[26] Religion teachers might convince their pupils that they can indeed *dare to hope*.

Notes

1. See W. Brueggemann, *The Bible and Post-modern Imagination*, pp. 24-25, 17-18.

2. I am very conscious of the fact that the four evangelists paint very distinctive portraits of Jesus, and that my Johannine picture needs to be complemented by images from the other Gospel writers. For an excellent treatment of this theme, see R. Schnackenburg, *Jesus in the Gospels: A Biblical Christology*.

3. See P. M. Devitt, *ID*, chapter 4, 'Building the Future in Hope', where I discuss the need 'to link past, present and future within the life of faith' (p. 43).

4. The proposed Leaving Certificate syllabus treats of 'The Death and Resurrection of Jesus' in Section B, *Christianity; Origins and Contemporary Expressions* (3.2).

5. 'Jesus as Messiah' is the title of the Leaving Certificate Section B, 2.5.

6. J. Gaffney, *Focus on Doctrine*, p. 93.

7. The Leaving Certificate Section G, *Worship, Prayer and Ritual* examines the meaning of sacrament (1.3).

8. D. Murray, *Jesus is Lord*, p. 85. For an account of the treatment of the sacraments in the *CCC*, see C. Gorman, 'The Seven Sacraments of the Church', in P. M. Devitt (ed.), *CC*.

9. H. Küng, *Eternal Life?*, p. 137.

10. See Leaving Certificate Section E, *Women, Religion and the Christian Tradition*, for a treatment of Mary, mother of Jesus (2.3).

11. Note how the Leaving Certificate syllabus deals with each of these major themes: for prayer, see Section G; for moral living, see Sections D and F; and for help in reading the Scriptures, see Section H.

12. See H. Küng, *EL?*, p. 145.

13. See the Leaving Certificate Section B, 2.4b.

14. H. Küng, quoting Moltmann, in *EL?*, p. 180.

15. See the Leaving Certificate Section D, 4.1d, 'the issue of freedom'.

16. See D. Murray, *JL*, chapter 5, 'The Law of Growth.'

17. Ibid., p. 13.

18 For a treatment of 'personal and social sin and the relationship between them' and 'the concept of structural injustice', see Leaving Certificate Section D, 2.3b, and c.

19 See Leaving Certificate Section A, 3.2, 'The concept of revelation'.

20 See Leaving Certificate Section D, 2.3a, for an examination of 'the Christian understanding of sin and reconciliation'.

21 Concern for 'the ecological crisis' is an integral part of the Leaving Certificate Section J, *Religion and Science* (2.4).

22 K. Rahner, *Theological Investigations*, Vol. 16, 'The foundations of belief today', p. 15.

23 See J. J. Haldane, 'The Need of Spirituality in Catholic Education', in J. C. Conroy (ed.), *Catholic Education Inside-Out/Outside-In* (Dublin: Veritas, 1999), p. 195: 'this very same Logos was incarnate in Jesus of Nazareth, the Way, the Truth and the Life. Thus are philosophy, history and spirituality united'.

24 See O. Maloney, 'Planning for a Future Church', *The Furrow* (March 1997), p. 135.

25 See K. Rahner, *Theological Investigations*, Vol. 7, 'Intellectual honesty and Christian Faith'.

26 See J. S. Marino (ed.), *BTRE*, p. ix.

Chapter 6

HOW TO GIVE AN IMAGINATIVE ACCOUNT OF THE FAITH?

Two young pals (one just beginning primary school, the other not yet in school) were playing at home one day.

'Let's play God', said Shane, the younger of the two.

'I'll be God', said Eoin, 'you can be my power-ranger'.

Eoin's mother overheard this conversation and listened attentively, out of sight, from the kitchen. A few minutes into the game she heard Shane ask, 'God, when you were being nailed to the cross, did it hurt?'

Eoin replied, 'Don't be silly, that wasn't me. That was my son, Jesus!'

This little episode, which happened in 1997, merits some reflection. The first thing that strikes one is that the Christian faith concerns a real historical figure. To be a Christian is, primarily, to live one's life in response to an historical figure (Jesus of Nazareth), and, only derivatively, the building up of a system of ideas (an ideology). Another thing that strikes one is how natural it is, even for very young children, to ask questions from within the experience of a lived faith, and also to offer good answers. One can sense here the emergence of both theological reflection (the questioning) and missionary preaching (the answering).

The fact that Christian faith is *historical, reflective and missionary* is very relevant to this topic, 'How to give an imaginative account of the faith?' Being historical means that Christianity is not primarily about ideas but primarily about historical characters, and therefore *story-telling* rather than explaining ideas is more suited to its propagation.[1]

However, even when the story has been well told, there usually comes a moment when *reflective questions* are put to the storyteller and he/she has to find new ideas and new images to make sense of the tale. And if the given answers fail to make sense, then further critical questions may flow. The human being is one who asks questions and looks for answers; but more than that, the human person also dares to question every given answer. That is why, even in primary school, Religion teachers are encouraged 'to teach their students religion with the same excitement and imagination as is currently being demonstrated in other curriculum areas'.[2] Many people say that this challenging approach to teaching Religion ought to continue all through second- and third-level education.[3]

This dialogical process of story-telling and being questioned and giving clearer answers is part of the *missionary dimension* of Christian faith. Being missionary is another way of saying that those who subscribe to the Christian faith cannot simply relax in its beauty and rejoice in its grace. They are summoned to share that grace and beauty with everybody. They must find ways to make sense of their faith, not just for themselves but also for those with whom they must speak.[4]

The need for inculturation
Uniting all these aspects gives rise to another dimension of Christian faith, namely *inculturation*. There is a shallow version of inculturation that merely touches the surface of life. It happened in post-independence Ireland when the existing English-style post-boxes were painted green instead of red. It happens also today in Scotland when the Prince of Wales wears a kilt on his visits there. If Christian faith were mere acceptance of an abstract idea, then this shallow form of inculturation would be possible: central Christian ideas would be clothed in some cultural garments. The Gospel and culture would merely be juxtaposed in some 'decorative manner'.[5]

However, the Christian faith is not just ideas. As we have seen in Chapter 5, it is faith in a historical Jewish person, Jesus of Nazareth, born of Mary, educated in Palestine, killed by Roman soldiers on Calvary, raised from death by the Father, believed in by faltering witnesses, proclaimed throughout the known world from then till now. In other words, Christian incarnational faith is, from its very heart, at its very core, in terms of its inner dynamic, already profoundly and unavoidably inculturated.[6] It also follows that, in the ongoing Christian mission to other cultures, the faith must be inculturated again and again. Christian faith must find ways in which the cultural strengths and weaknesses of all human races can dialogue with, be enriched by, and challenged to radical change by the Christian good-news story. This process of inculturating the Gospel has been, not just the changing of outward cultural trappings, but a movement of 'ongoing confrontation, assimilation and development'.[7] It has been a vital and profound process, 'going to the very roots of culture and the cultures of mankind'.[8]

The faith has been lived, understood, conceptualised and explained now for nigh on twenty centuries. It was first articulated and communicated in the concepts of the Semitic world, but soon was translated into the ideas of Greek philosophy. Clement of Alexandria organised a study circle in the late second century for Greek adults, whose sophisticated Hellenistic culture was the well from which he drew a language and images with which to teach them faith in Jesus Christ.[9] Thomas Aquinas made a bold attempt in the thirteenth century to explain the faith, not in terms of the traditional Platonic ideas, but rather in the newly discovered ideas of Aristotelian realism. Irish Christianity comprises many layers of successive inculturation, the most significant recent one laid down by the earthquake of the Great Famine.[10] Modern missionaries in Kenya have helped the local Masai people to rewrite the Nicene Creed in their own imaginative language.[11] Each age has had to grapple with new ways of understanding the world, and so each age has required of Christians that they rethink, reimagine and reconceptualise their faith in order to make it more accessible to new mentalities.[12]

Today's cultural climate

What are the major cultural assumptions of today? How can these shape the process of Christian self-reflection? These questions are at the heart of a provocative book by an Australian religious educator.[13] According to him, we live today out of a world view that is radically different from that of our ancestors in the faith. We have a new cosmology, and therefore need to give a new, creative, imaginative account of Christian faith that can be understood by the new mentality. Otherwise our faith will be judged to be unreal and irrelevant. The proposed Leaving Certificate RE syllabus assumes that the quest for meaning, that foundational human search, can be blocked or even fail to emerge in modern times because of certain cultural factors. One of these cultural factors is the oft perceived divergence between science and religion.

The syllabus faces this problem with courage. It does so in a very explicit manner in Section A (*The Search for Meaning and Values*) which is, in fact, the only obligatory section in the syllabus; and also in Section J (*Religion and Science*). Two particularly important elements to be noted here are the study of symbolic and metaphoric language in Section A, 2.1, and the 'issue-oriented' approach in Section J, 3 (*Current Issues for Religion and Science*). The approach throughout is to argue for a convergence between science and religion, in short, to point out how physics 'finds itself in a position similar to poetry and religion in that it must attempt to understand the unknown in terms of known models'.[14]

This syllabus material, if well handled, can only have a positive influence on the *intellectual* development of the faith of older teenagers.[15] It appears to take good account of what Gabriel Moran calls the 'disbelief' of young people and the fact that often their faith questions at this age have more to do with 'the external, verbal side of faith'[16] than the inner life of faith. In the language of Fritz Oser and Paul Gmünder, the syllabus recognises that 'religious judgement' is capable of refinement and development.[17] The syllabus respects the philosophical capacity of young adolescents and allows them to engage in 'concept cracking'.[18] It also seems to reflect the kind of 'searching faith' that has been noted in older teenagers and evidenced in some empirical studies.[19] Especially in the treatment of such issues as the origins of the universe, the life questions, and the genetics debate, it provides the stimulus for pupils to engage in 'informed debate' on these important issues and come to see the practical relevance as well as the truth of both religion and science.[20]

One key for understanding the convergence of religion and science is metaphorical thinking. Andrew McGrady has argued for 'the need to teach pupils to think religiously...in a way that takes account of the distinctive metaphorical nature of religious language', and he has also made a very perceptive comment that 'science, like the humanities and literature, is an affair of the imagination'.[21] What are at stake here are truth and its value for living. Can the truth be found in symbol and metaphor as well as in scientific hypothesis?[22] Can abstract scientific truth be relevant to issues of life and death? The proposed Leaving Certificate syllabus answers yes on both counts. In doing so, it seems to reflect an image of God as living music. While the religious person is happy to listen and enjoy the music and tell others to come along and enjoy it too, the scientist is prepared to analyse the mathematics of the music to see what its inner structure is. 'How our life would be changed if we could see that Greek geometry and the Christian faith have sprung from the same source!'[23] Good education should attend not only to the specific disciplines of knowledge but also to 'the unity of human knowledge'.[24] Thomas Curtis Clark expresses this point well in his poem, 'Faith and Science':

> Faith has no quarrel with science; she foreknows
> The truths which science grudgingly bestows.
> Believing David sang that God is one
> Ere science found one law in earth and sun.
> Faith knows no hindering bonds, she leaps to seize
> The truth which science doubts; the harmonies
> That men of science learned from age-long thought
> Were first revealed to hearts untrained, untaught,
> But reverent. Let faith from science learn
> Enduring patience; nor let science spurn
> The gift of faith, a never-failing love;
> Thus, each supporting each, the two shall prove
> The final truth of life, that God the Soul
> Through perfect law seeks perfect Beauty's goal.[25]

We have come a long way now from the story of five-year-olds asking profound theological questions. We have seen how older adolescents (soon to be young adults) will be challenged during their Leaving Certificate programme to make sense of the human search for meaning, and to join in the ongoing process of inculturation of the Christian religion. As pupils advance through the second-level schools, their ability to reason will usually advance beyond the constraints of concrete operations to the level of formal operations. They will become less tied to the world of sensory experience and begin to enter the world of abstract ideas. The new Junior Certificate syllabus is well aware of this intellectual development, and attempts to reflect it in different ways.

For example, in its explanation of the journal work that Junior Certificate pupils will submit as a significant part of their final assessment, the syllabus gives a list of the skills that journal work 'should draw on and promote' (p. 46). This list contains a wide range of intellectual abilities, such as inquiring, observing, problem-solving, researching, reflecting, organising and planning and evaluating critically. However, for fear one might expect too great a sophistication at this relatively early age, the syllabus links the journal work to a very manageable aim: 'to identify how understandings of…the Christian tradition have contributed to the culture in which we live, and continue to have an impact on personal life-style, inter-personal relationships etc'.

This is a task clearly within the ability of average Junior Certificate pupils. It also relates very well to three of the major aims of education as set forth in the *White Paper on Education* (1995, p. 10): 'to develop intellectual skills combined with a spirit of inquiry and the capacity to analyse issues critically and constructively; to develop expressive, creative and artistic abilities…; to foster a spirit of self-reliance, innovation, initiative and imagination'. These aims of general education will be well achieved by the intellectually stimulating programme of Religious Education now available at Junior Certificate level. Such a programme is well described in these terms: it offers pupils an opportunity 'to develop an informed and critical understanding of the Christian tradition in its historical origins and its cultural and social expressions…(and) to arrive at a thought-through moral stance that will serve as a foundation for the decisions they will face as adults' (*Junior Certificate Religious Education Syllabus*, p. 4).

The religious imagination

Here is another personal attempt to express imaginatively the core elements of the Christian faith, by considering the once very popular prayer called the Rosary. This traditional meditation is, of course, primarily a means of meditating on the mysteries of Jesus Christ and his Church. It once offered to illiterate medieval believers a suitable way of praying, when they could not understand the words of the classic prayers, the Psalms, and so could not join in praying the monastic office. However, just like the Nicene Creed, the Rosary can also function as a schematic and systematic account of the heart of Christian faith. When Josef Andreas Jungmann wrote so movingly about the Christocentrism of the faith, he was alluding not just to the person in whom Christians believe, but also to a unifying principle, whereby the whole diversity of beliefs, customs, traditions and theologies of the faith could be reduced to a certain unity.[26] Since people are gifted with minds that search for such unity, it is not surprising that many writings today stress its importance within the life of faith.[27]

How can the Rosary be seen as a schematic account of the heart of Christian faith, as a brief summary of the faith story? Provided it is imagined as a drama in three acts. Each act has an atmosphere – one is joyful, one is sorrowful, one full of the hope of glory. Each act in turn consists of five scenes – what are called 'mysteries'.[28]

Act 1: Joyful

The curtain rises on a young woman of courage and decision (the Annunciation scene). She is called Mary and she commits herself to the deepest possible involvement in the affairs of God and humanity. However, the main actor in this scene (though he is not yet seen) and the one to whom all the characters refer, is he who is called 'the son of the Most High' (Lk 1:32). In the second joyful scene there are numerous players but, once again, the spotlight is on him of whom it is said 'blessed is the fruit of your womb' (Lk 1:42). In the birth scene, while recognising Mary as mother, believers rejoice primarily in the 'Saviour, who is Christ the Lord' (Lk 2:11). The Presentation scene is also rich in players but no one doubts who is central. It is none other than the child who 'is set for the fall and rising of many in Israel' (Lk 2:34). In the finding scene, the key phrase consists of those challenging words which Luke, the dramatist, puts on the lips of his (now well-established) leading actor: 'did you not know that I must be in my Father's house?'

Act 2: Sorrowful

The second, sorrowful act begins in Gethsemani and passes, by many swift scene changes, to the courtyard of the fortress Antonia (where there is a pillar and where some thorn bushes grow); and from there through the narrow streets of Jerusalem to just outside the western wall, where there is a hillock called Calvary. These scenes portray the Son of the Most High, the fruit of Mary's womb, as he comes to the climax of his mission on earth. Mary, the woman of courage and decision, is to be found by her son's side – sad certainly, but ready even for new responsibilities. In this traumatic crucifixion scene she exemplifies a Christ-centred faith.

Act 3: Glorious

The Resurrection, the Ascension and the Descent of the Holy Spirit can be taken together. They form a meaningful unit, which could be referred to as Part 1 of the act of hope. The crucified, dead Jesus is now the glorified Christ finally established in his 'Father's house', not to be separated from his followers but in order to pour out upon them the life and power and joy and forgiveness of God's Holy Spirit. This is the glory that people meditate upon in the Rosary. But they also ponder the hope for humanity that this glory opens up. The Assumption and Coronation together form Part 2 of this final act. The basis for meditation is St Paul's letter to the Corinthians: 'For as in Adam all die, so also in Christ shall all be made alive. But each in his own order: Christ the first fruits, then at his coming those who belong to Christ' (1 Cor 15:22). In singling out Mary[29] for special mention here (*she* is Assumed and Crowned) there is no question of exclusivism. Since she has already been portrayed as the one who exemplifies Christian faith in Christ, it is only fitting that she be also mentioned as exemplifying Christian glorification in the Spirit. This is the hope held out to all those who believe in and belong to Christ, whether they be married or single, men or women, Jews or Greeks or barbarians, or Irish or African.

Reconceptualising the Christian faith

The Rosary is one very simple schematic representation or systematic exposition of the Christian faith. Many other approaches to reconceptualising the faith are possible. Artists have created beautiful icons and modern TV producers have taken this tradition further in their programming. Mystics have generated short prayers such as the 'Glory be'. Theologians have highlighted the value of pithy credal statements such as 'Jesus is Lord'. There is literally no end to the range of ways in which Christian believers have attempted to give an imaginative account of the faith they stand in, of the hope that sustains them and of the love that binds them to God and the whole human race.[30]

The American sociologist-novelist Andrew Greeley suggests a way of rereading the Nicene Creed so that it can be seen as a global response to some of the profound questions people ask out of their life experiences today. In doing this, he is accepting the intellectual challenge that faith must face in today's new world and attempting to re-interpret the Creed in an imaginative way. To show the continuity as well as the diversity of the Christian faith tradition, he attempts to link some typically modern questions to questions that are more typical of the Catechism tradition.[31] This can be seen in the following schematic representation:

1. Why did God make me?
2. Who was Jesus of Nazareth?
3. Is the Holy Spirit God?
4. Why did Jesus die on the Cross?
5. What is original sin?
6. What is sanctifying grace?
7. Is Jesus really present in the Holy Eucharist?
8. Is there salvation outside the Catholic Church?
9. Is there any way to be saved without baptism?
10. Is Mary truly the Mother of God?
11. After death, what happens to the good and evil?
12. When will the Last Judgement occur?

1. Is there any purpose in my life?
2. Are there any grounds for hope?
3. Is it safe to trust?
4. Why is there evil in the world?
5. Is human nature totally depraved?
6. Can our guilt be wiped away?
7. Is it possible to have friends?
8. Can there be unity among humankind?
9. Can we live in harmony with nature?
10. Can we find our sexual identity?
11. Why is life not fair?
12. Will we ever find peace?

Conclusion

A 'wisdom way of knowing' encourages people 'to use their minds, and their whole minds: reason indeed – its intuitive, logical and critical capacities – but also the depths of memory and the heights of imagination'.[32] Thinking profoundly and imaginatively about the faith can be exciting. Many great minds, and many lesser minds, have done it over and over again. And yet, there is no end to the possible questioning or the tentative answering or the re-thinking or the re-imagining. The humility of great science today in the face of a mysteriously exploding universe, is a lesson to religious thought as it probes the mystery of the Triune God. If taught in this spirit of joyful humility, the new Religious Education syllabuses will surely help young Irish pupils today to re-conceptualise and re-imagine their inherited faith, and so give a provocative account of the hope that is within them.

Notes

1. The centrality of storytelling will be highlighted later on, especially in Chapters 7 and 10, where I explore the Junior Certificate Section B, *Foundations of Religion – Christianity;* as well as the Leaving Certificate Section B, *Christianity: Origins and Contemporary Expressions;* Section I, Religion: *The Irish Experience;* and Section E, *Women, Religion and the Christian Tradition.*

2. See M. Ryan, 'Religious Education in Catholic Primary Schools', in *CSS,* 66, no. 1 (May 1993), p. 51.

3. See T. Hamill, 'An Open Letter to Educators', *The Furrow,* (Nov. 1992), pp. 617-619; and B. Watson, 'The Imagination and the Development of Religious Concepts', Chapter 5 of *ETRE.* Anne Holton assumes that Religion can be 'taught and examined in an active and imaginative way.' See 'Religious Education: an Examination Subject' in *The Furrow* (May, 2000) p. 293.

4. Other aspects of the missionary dimension of Christian faith will be dealt with when I examine the Junior Certificate Section C, *Foundations of Religion – Major World Religions;* and the Leaving Certificate Section C, *World Religions.*

5. See *GDC,* par. 204.

6. For an excellent exploration of 'the cultural milieu of the parables' of Jesus, see K. E. Bailey, *Poet and Peasant* and *Through Peasant Eyes: A Literary-Cultural Approach to the Parables of Luke,* p. 26. For a powerful linking of 'Incarnation' and 'Inculturation', see *GDC,* par. 109.

7. J. Dunne, 'Religion and Modernity: Reading the Signs' in E. G. Cassidy (ed.), *Faith and Culture in the Irish Context,* p. 131.

8. *GDC,* par. 204, quoting *Evangelii Nuntiandi,* 20.

9. See Clement of Alexandria, *Paidagogos* (Christ the Educator).

10. For an exploration of how Irish faith has been inculturated, see M. Drumm, 'Irish Catholics: A People Formed by Ritual', in E. G. Cassidy (ed.), *FCIC;* and *Passage to Pasch: Revisiting the Catholic Sacraments.*

11. See the text of the Masai creed in B. Marthaler, *The Creed,* p. 417.

12. See G. English, 'You're not speaking my language,' *CSS,* 65, no. 1 (May 1992).

13. M. Morwood, *Tomorrow's Catholic: Understanding God and Jesus in a New Millennium.*

14. See S. Mc Fague, *Metaphorical Theology*, p. 24. See also F. McCarthy, 'The Mind of God: Science and Theology Today', in E. G. Cassidy (ed.), *FCIC.*

15. See my treatment of religious knowledge (both factual and systematic) and the intellectual dimension of faith, in P. M. Devitt, *ID*, Chapter 2, 'Knowing God more clearly'.

16. See G. Moran, *Religious Education Development*, p. 151.

17. See F. Oser and P. Gmünder, *Religious Judgement: A Developmental Approach*, which talks of 'the deep-structures of religious judgement... [the] latently present patterns of religious consciousness which people use for coping with critical life-situations' (p. 33).

18. See T. Cooling, *Concept Cracking: Exploring Christian Beliefs in School*, p. 8.

19. See especially P. Fahy, *FCC*, p. 115.

20. See M. Crawford and G. Rossiter, 'The Secular Spirituality of Youth: Implications for Religious Education', *BJRE*, 18, no. 3 (Summer 1996), p. 136.

21. See A. McGrady, 'Glimpsing the Divine: Metaphor and Religious Thinking', in Lane (ed.), *RCD*, pp. 178, 158.

22. For an exposition of the sources of tension between science and religion, especially within school, see M. C. Poole, 'Science and Religion in the Classroom', in L. Francis and A. Thatcher (eds.), *CPFE.*

23. S. Weil, *Gateway to God*, p. 147.

24. L. Newbigin, 'Religion, science and truth in the school curriculum', in L. Francis and A. Thatcher (eds.), *CPFE*, p. 98.

25. See T. C. Clark, *1000 Quotable Poems.*

26. See J. A. Jungmann, *The Good News Yesterday and Today.*

27. See *GCD*, pars. 38-45; *Catechesi tradendae*, pars. 5, 6, 21; K. Nichols, *Cornerstone*, pars. 125-128; J. Finley and M. Pennock, *Your Faith and You;* K. Rahner, *Theological Investigations*, Vol. 9, 'The need for a short formula of Christian Faith'; and Vol. 11, 'Reflections on the problems involved in devising a short formula of the faith'.

28. There are clear echoes here of the medieval mystery play.

29. For an exposition of the place of Mary in Irish Spirituality, see M. Maher (ed.), *Irish Spirituality*, Chapter 4; also P. O'Dwyer, *Mary: A History of Irish Devotion* and 'Mary in the Irish Tradition', in J. Hyland (ed.), *Mary in the Church*.

30. For a masterly account of the four languages of faith, 'story' and 'liturgy' (which tilt more towards experience) and 'doctrine' and 'morality' (which are more distanced from experience), see K. Nichols, *Refracting the Light: Learning the Languages of Faith*, p. 22.

31. See A. Greeley, *The Great Mysteries*.

32. T. Groome, *EFL*, pp. 289-90.

Chapter 7

WHY TEACH CHURCH HISTORY?

In exploring the *intellectual* dimension of faith in the last chapter, I pointed out that Christian faith is historical, reflective and missionary. I concentrated primarily on the latter two processes, reflection and mission, as demands of Christian faith. It is time now to give greater attention to the *historical* nature of Christianity.

My question here is, 'Why teach Church history?' There are three main reasons. The first is *cultural,* and will make sense no matter who is learning. For both Christian believers and non-Christians, it is worthwhile studying Church history to realise and appreciate its effects for good and for ill on world politics, art, music, literature, etc. This is the study of Christian history from a purely cultural perspective. It is precisely this kind of study that is encouraged by the Junior Certificate RE syllabus, when it notes that 'the history of humanity has been indelibly marked by the contributions of religious traditions' and that 'in Ireland, Christianity is part of our rich cultural heritage'. Accordingly, young Irish people during their education at school should be introduced to 'the values – moral, spiritual, religious, social and cultural – which have been distinctive in shaping Irish society' (p. 3).

There are two other reasons for studying Church history, and these apply only to believers. One is *theological,* the other is *ecumenical.*

The *theological* reason for studying Church history springs from two key truths of Christian faith, namely, Incarnation and Trinity. Michael Himes, reflecting carefully on these two mysteries of Christian faith, has pointed out that Christianity began on earth in the scandalous particularity of Jesus of Nazareth; and has managed to come down to us today *only* through the power of the good-news story told by people who knew the risen Lord Jesus. Apart from these people (the Church), the world 'would have no knowledge of God in Christ'.[1] Ideas, in principle, could be passed down in a book. But a person can be communicated only through personal witness. Ideas might well live on without people. But Christianity does not really exist apart from believing people. Furthermore, the God of Jesus Christ is a communion of persons, and a glimpse of this Triune God can best be caught from looking at a mirror-image human community of believers. Reasoning thus, Himes came to the conclusion that we need the Church. I would go further and say: the better to tell of Jesus and the sharper to mirror God, not only do we need the Church but we also need to teach Church history.

The *ecumenical* reason for studying Church history flows from the existing disunity of Christians, which mocks the prayer of Jesus, blocks the vision of God, and is truly a scandal to the world.[2] It is a central task of Christian believers today to engage in ecumenical dialogue. In preparing for this task, believers can be helped if they know where the divisions come from. In this sense, history may be not only a great teacher but also a great healer of wounds.

The historical content of the new RE syllabuses

Junior Certificate pupils will probably all take Section A (*Communities of Faith*). Here they will be introduced to an interesting dialectic between 'today' and 'yesterday'. History will be shown to relate as much to the present as to the distant past. Beginning with 'communities of faith today' in Ireland, pupils will then move on to listen to the 'stories of the earliest followers and their leaders' (p. 11). But they will return once again to today's world and will explore in depth 'the relationships between different communities of faith and particularly between different Christian denominations in Ireland' (p. 12). The relevance of this material for ecumenical dialogue and inter-religious debate is obvious.

In Junior Certificate Section B (*Foundations of Religion – Christianity*), a similar 'then and now' pattern is obvious. The historical context in which Jesus lived is explicitly dealt with, as are the historical sources for evidence of his life (pp. 15-16). And when 'the person and preaching of Jesus' are dealt with (p. 17) they are related not just to his disciples then but also to his followers today. There is also a section dealing with 'the first Christian communities' (p. 19), which examines how their identity emerged and how their community life developed. However, and this comes somewhat as a surprise, there is nothing at all concerning the growth of Christianity after the early phase until today. There is nothing corresponding to Part 4 of Section C (*Major World Religions*), which traces the 'development of tradition' (p. 24). I shall be suggesting later on some ways for teachers of Catholic pupils to make good this omission.

The proposed Leaving Certificate RE syllabus shows a keen awareness of the need for an historical perspective on religion *in general*. In Section E (*Women, Religion and the Christian Tradition*), a key 'attitudinal objective' is an 'appreciation of the contribution of women to religious and spiritual traditions'. In Section H (*The Bible: Literature and Sacred Text*), pupils are introduced to 'the three phases of the historical narratives' of the Hebrew scriptures (part 2.1d) and are required to ask of the Gospels, are they 'historical narrative or testimony of faith?' (part 2.2c). Section J (*Religion and Science*) contains an historical treatment of 'the relationship between Religion and Science' (part 2) from the time of Galileo down to today, with special reference to Newton, Descartes and Darwin.

A similar lively historical perspective is also present in the specific treatment of the Christian tradition. One of the 'understanding objectives' of Section B (*Christianity; Origins and Contemporary Expressions*) is that the students will 'be aware of the historical nature of Christianity and the role of the cultural context in the shaping of belief and practice from ancient times to the present day'. In articulating the vision, life, death and resurrection of Jesus as prime founder of Christianity, Section B 2 situates Jesus and his teachings within the religious, political and cultural contexts in which they arose. The treatment of the first Christian communities in B 4 allows pupils to sense the variety of historical memories coming down from the early Christian movement.

The *ecumenical* potential of such study is hinted at in a fine book by Raymond Brown, in which he analyses the New Testament, in order to lay bare the variety of ecclesiological emphases in different Churches, e.g. a body with structure, Christ's body to be loved, a Spirit-filled body, the People of God, people personally attached to Jesus, individuals guided by the Paraclete-Spirit, authority that does not stifle Jesus. Speaking as a Roman Catholic, he writes: 'It is a strength for a Church like mine to preserve the emphasis on sound teaching authority in the Pastorals; but such a Church may need to examine itself about the role that John gives to the Paraclete-Spirit as a teacher dwelling in each Christian'.[3]

The central importance of 'returning to origins as a pattern in Christianity' is clearly recognised in part 1.1c of this historical Section B. But this is not enough, it seems to me, and it would be wise for Religion teachers of Catholic pupils to *supplement* the many concrete examples already given in the proposed Leaving Certificate syllabus with some other modern examples of vibrant Christian community, that draw inspiration from Christian origins. One such example would be the community of Sant' Egidio in Rome. Another would be the worldwide community of L'Arche.[4]

A sense of one *particular* Christian history enlivens Section I (*Religion: The Irish Experience*), especially part 3.2 'Key elements of the Irish experience of Christianity' and also part 4.2 'Recent changes in Religion in Ireland'. The syllabus material here could well be *supplemented* by many other graphic examples of Christian community experience in modern Ireland.[5] One of the hoped for effects of this historical presentation of the Christian faith is that students will develop a greater historical understanding and thereby be better equipped to engage in ecumenical dialogue today and in the unending 'search for Christian unity' (Section B, 5.2).

Such historical studies as are envisaged by the new syllabuses are very worthwhile for Catholic pupils, even at the cultural level of pure knowledge and understanding. In general, it is better to be knowledgeable than to be ignorant. It is better to understand than to be perplexed. But this is not the principal reason why Catholic teenagers ought to study Church history. As mentioned above, Christianity is not primarily a list of ideas and abstract truths (to be recorded in books); its very meaning is essentially historical (it celebrates, not primarily religious ideas, but the good-news story of the inbreaking of God in the historical person of Jesus of Nazareth). If it were merely an ideology, it would be possible to pass it on mainly through books or other media. Since it is essentially an historical movement, books alone will never suffice. Only particular people (believers) can tell the good news of the scandalously particular Jesus

Christ. And because the God of Jesus Christ is a communion-God, only a living human community (often called the Church Universal or the Great Tradition) can sustain the life and witness of such believers. This it does by functioning as 'a great communal wellspring... a great river of vitality'.[6]

Need to supplement the new syllabuses

Given their nature, as State-sponsored syllabuses, which may not favour any particular Christian or religious point of view, the new syllabuses cannot be expected to subscribe to the Catholic understanding of living tradition just outlined above by providing a fully comprehensive Catholic history. From the point of view of Catholic RE, this is where the main weakness of the syllabus lies. While studying the new syllabus will be helpful to teenage Catholics in gaining *some* valid historical and ecumenical perspectives, if they are to be adequately taught Church history, then the typical Catholic school will need to offer (over and above these new syllabuses) a much larger and broader historical perspective of Catholic faith.[7] This could be done by offering a substantial historical component in each year's Religion course. The need for such a provision follows inexorably from another inherent weakness in the proposed Leaving Certificate syllabus, from the point of view of teenage Catholics. Even if they study this syllabus, they are *not* obliged to study Section B (*Christianity; Origins and Contemporary Expressions*).

How can Catholic schools ensure that the entire RE curriculum has an adequate historical component? Crawford and Rossiter have argued strongly for the setting up of an historical core to the second-level RE curriculum.[8] Here is the outline of their proposal. The curriculum contains three sections, corresponding with early, middle and late secondary (roughly 12-14, 14-16 and 16-18 years of age). The historical material is sequential: (a) It begins with the Old Testament and New Testament foundations of the early Church. At this stage of schooling, pupils are still curious enough to want to know the background facts; (b) In the middle period, the medieval Church, the Reformation and Counter-Reformation are major themes. Pupils at this age are often rebellious enough to be able to empathise with some of the major historical figures of this era; (c) In senior cycle, the main topic is the Church in the changing, modern world. The greater intellectual maturity of pupils can now be brought to bear on the role of religion in modern life and religion's contribution to modern social and political issues.

Another possible approach to developing an historical core to the RE syllabus would be to enlist the support of interested history teachers and, drawing on their critical and professional skills, to compose two story-lists: a list of positive and a list of negative aspects of Christian history over two thousand years.[9] By exposing young pupils to both lists over the entire period of schooling, the Religion teachers would enable them to sail smartly between the Scylla of subtle indoctrination ('we are thoroughly good') and the Charybdis of culpable ignorance ('I never knew that').

Justifying an historical core curriculum in second-level RE

I shall now attempt to justify the setting up of an historical core to second-level RE, as one way of handling content in Religion teaching. Two preliminary remarks must be made: first, regarding the overall aims of Religion teaching; and, second, regarding the Religion teacher's stance *vis-à-vis* Religion during the RE class:

(1) I assume here, what has been argued already, that the most suitable manner of teaching Religion in second-level classrooms is through an open, enquiring study of Religion.[10] This means that the Religion teacher sets out to help the pupils have an educational encounter with religion. The main aims of teaching Religion in second-level classrooms are to give information about religion, and to develop in pupils the necessary emotional skills to help them to empathise with people of religious faith and the intellectual skills to think critically about religion, both in the world and in their own lives.

(2) I am advocating here that the Religion teacher and pupils need to adopt a stance of limited distancing from the experience of religion, during the teaching of Religion in class. How then might this kind of Religion teaching also involve a personal dimension? My answer is, through the imagination. A curriculum of RE built around an historical core could be as dry as dust, and lacking a personal tone, unless it were taught imaginatively.[11] As long as the historical teaching were sufficiently detailed, it would provide adequate factual content to

enable pupils to identify imaginatively with historical figures and to rehearse imaginatively the values these figures have revealed. To visit 'those prophetic places where the Church finds itself as a broken body among poor and afflicted people'[12] must surely be, for pupils, both an enriching and an enlightening experience. Imaginative rehearsal is not meant as a substitute for knowledge, but rather as an enhancement of knowledge.

There are *four* parts to my case. I shall argue for an historical core to the Religion curriculum from the needs of the school principal, from the needs of the teachers of Religion and from the needs of the pupils. I shall conclude by arguing from the needs of today.

(1) Imagine yourself as a *school principal*. Your school has twenty-four classes. They all have three periods of Religion each week. You want your pupils to receive a challenging, comprehensive religious education in school. You need to have at your disposal a map of the complete RE journey to be taken by the pupils as they progress through school. Two such maps are the schemas just mentioned above. Once these have been accepted by the staff, then you can ask one teacher to walk thus far, another teacher to tread warily in this area, another teacher to cover ground quickly at a certain stage, and so on. When each teacher knows in advance where other teachers are operating, there need be no unnecessary overlapping of content, no muddy paths that everyone has walked on while other pathways are untrodden. The content of such RE will always be fresh and challenging, comprehensive and enlightening.

(2) Now think of yourself as a *Religion teacher* in that school. What advantage is there for you in such an historical core curriculum? The following: you have a curriculum that is teachable. Instead of naming the content in devotional terms ('our response to God'; 'praying the Rosary', etc.), an historical core curriculum names its contents in teachable terms ('the impact of religion on social morality'; 'the role of repetitive praying in the great world religions', etc.) The aims of each year are quite specific. The central ideas are clearly articulated. You can search for suitable resources and plan suitable assessment strategies to evaluate the content your pupils have learnt.

(3) Imagine you are one of *the pupils* who say 'we've done all that Religion stuff before'. What you need is a Religion curriculum that

will move along into fresh areas of life without unnecessary repetition of content. At primary school you will have heard about Jesus and will have listened to many of his parables. How can you learn any new content about Jesus at second level, without boring repetition? You could, for example (and all the textbooks do this already), explore, in early second level, the geographical, historical and religious background against which Jesus lived. At that stage you are inquisitive and willing to explore. In the middle years of second level, when you may be rebellious and argumentative, you could build on this basis by examining some classic followers of Jesus (the saints) and studying them as resistance fighters in the war against evil. This is valuable new content, which is indirectly related to the key theme of Jesus. At senior level you are more reflective, more philosophical in outlook. This would be a suitable time to make a critical, historical study of the person of Jesus: what sort of person he was, his main values, how he dealt with people, how his life inspired some and antagonised others, etc. In other words, at different stages of second-level schooling you will have learnt new content regarding an ancient theme.

(4) *The period we live in* has been marked by big changes in the Church. The old people remember what it used to be like. The young can barely imagine it. Some have never even heard of Pope John XXIII. A major role for RE in a time of change and upheaval is surely to help people retain their foothold, but also to offer them opportunities to move ahead. In other words, RE has both conservative and critical functions.[13] I know of nothing better than a study of history to help us retain our equilibrium in a changing world and gently move us to become, in our turn, critical agents of future change.

A practical example of historical content in RE[14]

Here is an example of what might be involved in teaching one particular religious topic as part of a curriculum with an historical core. The topic is the Rosary. What tends to happen to this topic nowadays? Some Religion teachers see it on the programme but skip it because they don't like it, and they only teach whatever Christian content they believe in strongly. Other teachers pray the Rosary devoutly every day; so they think nothing of appealing to their pupils to take this devotion and make it their own. This approach may often backfire, since the content of personal devotion does not transfer so easily. Other teachers may have no time for the Rosary, but still exhort their pupils to pray it daily, because this seems to be the school policy. Such teaching is almost devoid of content.

There is another, more educationally sound way of teaching the Rosary. This involves an exploration of what the Rosary has meant for Catholics in the past, what it means for Catholics today, and what might be the future of the Rosary. The process could enfold like this. The teacher could give an historical outline of the devotion. The pupils could then do some research by interviewing parents and older Catholics about the Rosary in their lives and by writing reports on their findings. The teacher could then explain how other world religions have similar kinds of repetitive, mantra-like devotions. The pupils could be given an experience of praying the Rosary in the school prayer-room, after some instruction regarding different ways of praying. Afterwards they could do a written assignment on the strengths and weaknesses of this kind of devotion. A class discussion could then follow. The teacher might then be able to comment that, while the Rosary is not a regular devotion in his/her own life, there are times, like funerals, when it is a great support. Some pupils might even be enabled by this serious study of the Rosary to describe how their own attitude to it has changed. To aim *directly* at personal faith-sharing within the classroom may prevent its ever happening. To allow it to flow naturally from the serious study of content would seem to be the best approach.

This is one example of a respectful and enriching encounter with religious content. It is far removed from proselytising or indoctrination, which appeal to the emotions while bypassing the mind. It is one good way of making the religious traditions of a historical Church accessible to young people without pressuring them into taking up a particular practice. History can indeed be a great teacher. It can also be of inestimable value in the organising of teachable content.

It was not by accident that I chose to explore a Marian theme in this chapter. One of the great 'myths' of the past was that Mary belonged to Catholics while, in general, Protestants had little time for

Marian devotion. Like all 'myths', this contained some truth, but it also obscured some elements of reality. One powerful way of exploding such damaging 'myths' and half truths, and fostering a greater *ecumenical* spirit among young Catholic teenagers today, would be to move beyond such an historical study of the Rosary and to read a work on Mary by a leading Anglican scholar of today.[15]

Conclusion

'What do you mean by religion? Do you mean the way it is or the way God intended it to be? There's a big difference, you know.'[16] Pupils today need help to deal creatively with this kind of debate regarding Church history. The historical content of the NCCA syllabus is a very welcome addition to the stock of ideas for teaching the Christian faith as an historical reality. Furthermore, it should help to foster in young people that ongoing understanding of faith-differences that lies at the heart of ecumenical dialogue. However, given that no State-sponsored syllabus can easily reflect the fullness of any specific Christian tradition, Catholic pupils would also benefit from exposure to complementary material and additional courses, such as those mentioned above.[17]

Notes

1. See M. Himes, 'Why do we need a Church?', in *The Furrow* (March 1997), p. 265.
2. See P. M. Devitt, *ID*, Chapter 7: 'Working for Christian Unity'.
3. R. Brown, *The Churches the Apostles Left Behind*, p. 149.
4. See J. Vanier, *Community and Growth*, p. 4.
5. See J. O'Brien, *Seeds of a New Church*, especially Part 2.
6. See T. Groome, *EFL*, p. 256
7. This point is forcefully made in the new *GDC*, par. 30, which notes how 'reference to Sacred Scripture is virtually exclusive and unaccompanied by sufficient reference to the Church's long experience and reflection, acquired in the course of her two-thousand-year history'.
8. See M. Crawford and G. Rossiter, *TRSS*, Part 2; and also *MTC*, Chapter 17.
9. See T. W. Tilley, *Story Theology*, especially Chapter 8, 'The Body of Christ'; M. Sawicki, *The Gospel in History;* and J. O'Donohue, *Anam Chara*.
10. See the earlier chapter, 'What is the main purpose of the Religion class?'
11. Hence the importance of 'nurturing a historical imagination', as described in W. Brueggemann, *The Bible Makes Sense*, pp. 25-37.
12. See J. Dunne, 'Religion and Modernity: Reading the Signs', in E. G. Cassidy (ed.), *RCIC*, p. 135.
13. See P. M. Devitt, 'The Challenge of Religious Education', *Doctrine and Life* (March 2000), p. 157.
14. See M. Crawford and G. Rossiter, *op. cit.*
15. J. Macquarrie, *Mary for all Christians*.
16. J. F. Girzone, *Joshua*, p. 73
17. An overview of Papal History is available in E. Duffy, *Saints and Sinners: A History of the Popes*.

Chapter 8

WHY TEACH WORLD RELIGIONS?

In recent years the teaching of Religion in Irish schools has seen many changes. One of the most striking is the introduction of significant content dealing with the great world religions, both at junior and senior cycle. The two new RE syllabuses also offer substantial material on the great world religions. Section C in Junior Certificate aims 'to explore in detail a major world religion', e.g. Buddhism, Hinduism, Islam or Judaism (p. 20). A noteworthy aspect of this fine Section is that it regularly invites teachers and pupils to pay particular attention to what might be called 'the Irish connection', in other words, to study the great world religions not just as something foreign and exotic, but 'with particular reference to followers in Ireland' (p. 25). However, it is still a matter of debate among many Religion teachers to what extent this kind of teaching is either necessary or even possible. There are many voices that need to be heard in relation to this topic. Therefore, in this chapter I shall consider both the case *against* and the case *for* trying to teach the great world religions at second level.

'I don't know anything about them'.
This *is* a genuine problem, but only initially. If the teacher approaches personal ignorance, not as a block to teaching, but as a *challenge* to learn for oneself, then some of the excitement and freshness that comes from making one's own discoveries could help the teacher motivate the pupils in the same direction. The importance attached by the new Junior Certificate syllabus to the study of the great world religions can be deduced from a close reading of the document. The first obvious point that strikes one is that there is a very substantial Section (C) dealing specifically with *Major World Religions.*

Not so obvious perhaps, but very significant, is the fact that in Section A (*Communities of Faith*), which most pupils will probably take, there is also a certain amount of material dealing with the great world religions. This is to ensure that those students not taking Section C will at least be 'able to retell stories about the founders/ earliest followers of Buddhism, Christianity, Hinduism, Islam and Judaism' (p. 11). Furthermore, in each of the Sections D, E and F, there are specific references to more than one religious tradition: pupils are meant to 'be able to identify evidence of religious belief in stories from two religious traditions' (p. 30); they are supposed to look too 'at important people in the spiritual traditions' (p. 37) of the different religions; and study how different religions lead to different ways of thinking morally (p. 42).

'There are no suitable resources to teach them adequately'.
Lack of resources is always a problem in teaching. However, the situation is not as bad as it seems. Many easily accessible journals such as *The Irish Catechist, Doctrine and Life, Religious Education* and the *British Journal of Religious Education* have published numerous articles over the past three decades which deal with issues in the teaching of all the great world religions.[1] These articles often provide lists of teacher and pupil resources, as well as references to educational films, tapes and videos.

Though the Jewish origins of the Christian faith are well dealt with in many existing Religion textbooks, one area that gets very little treatment is post-Christian Judaism. It's as if, once Christianity arrived, there was no need to examine the ongoing Jewish traditions. However, one fine Australian textbook by Crawford and Rossiter attempts to fill this lacuna.[2] The programme for year 10 (sixteen-year-olds) shows how modern Judaism is a vibrant faith in spite of anti-Semitism and the Holocaust. The proposed Leaving Certificate syllabus Section C, 2, requires that honours students undertake a 'study of the relationship between Christianity and Judaism'. One hopes that the relationship that exists *today* between both these great religious traditions will be examined seriously in Irish schools.

Crawford and Rossiter's *TRSS* also examines Buddhism, with reference especially to the topic of human suffering.[3]

In the context of what the proposed Leaving Certificate Section C, 1.2, calls 'primal religion', the *TRSS* year 12 treatment of the Aboriginal religion might be considered too exotic for many classrooms in Ireland. However, since this Australian religion has much in common with our own Celtic religion, especially in regard to respect for the land,[4] perhaps even a modest awareness of these two older religions might be of benefit to sophisticated late-twentieth-century humanity. The ecological perspective of ancient Irish religion is clearly visible in Leaving Certificate Section I (*Religion: The Irish Experience*), part 3.2a, which deals with 'the sacral character of the land'.

Perhaps the most interesting factor to note with regard to *TRSS* is that it offers two distinct chapters on Islam (one for fifteen-year-olds, the other for seventeen-year-olds). Taken together, these chapters offer an ongoing teaching that respects pupils' growing critical awareness and their more penetrating questioning ability.

A fine modern Irish textbook that deals sensitively with all the great world religions and could be very helpful for those teaching these topics for the first time, is *World Religions and Belief*, by Fleming and O'Hara.[5]

Worth mentioning here too is the New Zealand Catholic school RE syllabus, *Understanding Faith*, which examines every topic each year from seven different angles, one of which is called the 'Universal Religious Dimension'.[6]

'Parents will not thank you for trying to convert their children to another religion'.

A Religion teacher in an Irish second-level school was once asked by an interested pupil, 'Are you an Islam?' Perhaps the pupil felt the teacher was proselytising. However, when an *open* study of world religions is undertaken, as I have already indicated in Chapter 3, this open study means that no faith response is being directly aimed at in class. The purpose of such study is not to convert pupils, nor even to give reasons to pupils explaining why they might want to convert to Islam. The aims of such teaching are rather to give knowledge about Islam and develop such skills for studying Religion as will lead to greater understanding of and a richer feeling for Islam. The aim is to help pupils get into the shoes of Islam. No Islamic faith is assumed either in the pupils or in the teacher. What is assumed is a readiness and a firm commitment to making an honest, fair and appreciative study of one of the world's great religions.[7] This is also the perspective of the new RE syllabus for Junior Certificate: 'The aim of Junior Cycle Religious Education is to provide students with a framework for encountering and engaging with the variety of religious traditions in Ireland and elsewhere' (p. 4). Students will then, hopefully, 'appreciate the richness of religious traditions' (p. 5) other than their own.

'How can a Christian make any sense of these other religions?'

To make sense of Islam[8] one could try to study it from a totally objective and scientific point of view. Few people today believe in this kind of total objectivity. 'Even contemporary philosophy of science recognises that the idea of the detached observer is dead'.[9] This approach would not take one very far, because no religion allows of such an analysis. Its riches would slip through the holes of one's analytical nets. To make sense of Islam one could, of course, convert to the religion, live with it, and in this way come to understand it better. Nobody is suggesting such a radical approach.

But there *is* another way to study Islam. It is what I call *study from a distance*. It realises that one's own religious experience of life (as a Catholic) gives one a feel for and a knowledge of many *common* religious factors, such as prayer, fasting, helping the poor, etc. Being rooted in Catholic life makes one very different in *specific* detail from Muslim people. It means that one is removed from Islam, at a distance from Islam in regard to *specific* details of faith. But one also has an experience of *common ground* with Islam, being religious oneself, and this is a help rather than a hindrance in studying Islam. I find it fascinating to reflect on the fact that Sections B (*Christianity*) and C (*Major World Religions*) of the Junior Certificate are structurally very similar. There is a clear assumption here, it seems to me, that pupils' learning about Christianity can be helped if they adopt a similar approach to learning about other religions; and vice versa.

In attempting to study Islam, one need not fear being committed to Catholicism. Such a commitment is merely evidence of our 'humanly unavoidable partiality'; and that is why such a faith commitment 'constitutes the teacher's primary and most valuable resource'.[10] Rather than fearing commitment to one faith as a block to respectful teaching of another, the Junior Certificate syllabus regularly recommends that teachers and pupils try to study two religious traditions at the same time; examples would be the following: 'stories of faithful people from two religious traditions' (p. 30); 'recognising the religious symbols of other religious traditions' (p. 36); 'the moral visions of two major world religions, one of which should be Christianity' (p. 38); and 'examining how two different religious moral visions contribute to the decision-making of believers' (p. 42).

A similar methodology is obvious in the proposed Leaving Certificate Section C, 2, which takes 'a closer look at the major living (religious) traditions', and assumes that it is both possible and beneficial to study two religious traditions *together*. Comparisons are supposed to be made between the images of God found in the two traditions, the vision of salvation/liberation proposed by the two traditions, the importance of community in the two traditions, and elements of rite in the two traditions. The image of the fair-wheel might help here.[11] Being off the horse, but still on the roundabout, is like studying religion from a certain distance. Being off the roundabout, but still on the common earth, is like the study of Religion by non-religious people.

'I couldn't teach Islam, because I detest the way it treats women'.
The kind of study of Islam that is being advocated here is *firstly* a non-evaluative study. In other words, its aim is to learn as much as possible about Islam. Metaphorically, it means taking off one's shoes, showing respect for what is other, in order to understand it better. At a *later* stage of the study, when pupils are more mature, it would also be possible to do an evaluative study of Islam. This would mean comparing it to other religions and passing some tentative judgements about it. Or one could try to evaluate it from within its own terms of reference: how consistent are its practices with its stated creed? The proposed Leaving Certificate Section E, 1.2, which examines 'the place of women in the sacred texts and living traditions of different religions' should provide much helpful insight for older pupils as they attempt such evaluations.

'We have the truth. What can these other religions teach us?'
We may think we *have* the truth. It would be more accurate to say that God's truth has us. We are the gifted ones, because God has given us

in Jesus the way, the truth and the life. We do not possess Jesus the truth. We are possessed by him, enveloped in his revelation. This is the heart of our Christian faith. And it explains the essential missionary thrust of the Christian faith.[12] Christians inevitably seek to share their good experience of the Father God and God's Son and God's Spirit with others. There is an essential 'outreach' dimension to Christian faith, a sense that all Christian believers ought to reach out to the whole world, in speaking their startling good news about God's love in Christ. In the Christian 'mission to reveal the ultimate possibility for humanity' *every* believer has a part to play; 'there is indeed no place for idleness'.[13] The notion of a vibrant missionary Church is well expressed in these words: 'the church is the only society in the world which exists for the sake of those who are not members of it'.[14]

But it is also an integral part of that same Christian faith, as articulated in the Second Vatican Council, that in many other mysterious ways, the Lord Jesus is communicating his truth to others who do not belong to the Christian faith. If one has eyes to see and ears to listen, one can recognise the seeds of the Gospel in all the world's great religions: for example, Islam's submission to God as the heart and pulse of religion; Hinduism's concern for all living creatures; and Buddhism's emphasis on prayerful meditation. Western believers could also learn from the religions of the East the central importance of 'the intuitive mind'[15] in the life of faith. It is very gratifying to notice that the Junior Certificate RE syllabus wants pupils to 'understand the meaning of inter-faith dialogue' (p. 12), presumably so that their minds and hearts would be opened up to learning from such dialogue throughout their lives.

All of the great world religions are part of God's truth, and can reveal to Christian believers some of the mysterious face of God. They can be for Christians a modern epiphany of God. Many returned Christian missionaries would confirm this point of view. Notice, too, how well the proposed Leaving Certificate Section A appreciates the need for sensitivity among Christians towards the other great world religions. One of the 'attitude-objectives' of this Section (*The Search for Meaning and Values*) is entitled 'critical awareness of and sensitivity to the variety of religious responses'.

'There'll be less time available for teaching the Catholic religion'.
It is true that, if one studies Islam, there will be less time available to
study Christianity. This need not be such a bad thing, however. It is
not so much the amount of time that is crucial here as the *quality* of
the teaching and learning that happens in the shorter period of time.
It is possible that exposure to a serious study of Islam might have a
positive impact on the quality of Religion teaching in general. *Firstly*,
if the teaching of Islam is done in such a way that pupils realise no
faith response is being directly aimed at, then over time they could
well experience precisely that freedom of enquiry about Religion and
religious matters that can sometimes be missing in the study of their
own Religion. If this were to happen, they might realise it is also
possible to study their own Religion without feeling they are going to
be brainwashed while doing it. The shorter time available to study
Catholicism might be a blessing in disguise. It might be qualitatively
better than if Islam were not also being taught.

Secondly, such a study of Islam would introduce pupils to aspects of
religious life with which they are not yet familiar. The *newness* of the
content might even suggest to them that it is worthwhile to look again
in an open way at their own Religion. Often the motivation to study
their own Religion is low, because familiarity breeds contempt. In a
paradoxical way, by highlighting the freshness of Religion, the study of
Islam might contribute to a fresh study of Christianity.

Young Christians might learn to understand better their own belief
in only *one* God, the value of regular daily *prayer* (did St Dominic copy
the rosary beads from Islam?), the centrality of concern for the *poor*,
the religious motivation to *fasting*, and something of the paradox of
religious *pilgrimages*. Some of these issues are specifically mentioned in
different parts of the proposed Leaving Certificate Syllabus. For
example, Section A (*The Search for Meaning and Values*) in part 3.1c
examines 'the concepts of God in the monotheistic traditions of
Judaism, Christianity and Islam'; Section F (*Issues of Justice and Peace*)
in part 2.3b examines 'the Zakat of Islam'; and Section G (*Worship,
Prayer and Ritual*) in part 2.3c studies 'places of prayer' (including a
mosque), while part 3.2d explores 'pilgrimage, poustinia and retreat'.

'What's the point of teaching about religions that are tied up with outdated cultures?'

It depends on what is meant by 'outdated'. The old Celtic religion of Ireland had a great conviction of life after death. The even more ancient Aboriginal religion of Australia has a beautiful regard for the sacredness of the land. In the context of studying the proposed Leaving Certificate Section F (*Issues of Justice and Peace*), insights gleaned from this ancient Aboriginal religion could easily complement material in parts 3c and 3d: 'the creation texts in Genesis and the concepts of stewardship and domination', and 'the consequences of these interpretations for the earth and the environmental crises'. Though certain religions may be outdated, they still remain invaluable.

'Members of other religions (e.g. Muslims) would resent Catholics teaching Islam'.

If members of other religions show resentment, teachers need to examine their conscience. Maybe their teaching is not careful, or too judgemental or too dismissive of the religion in question. Maybe they are too uncritical of the religion in question!

Strong reasons for studying World Religions

There are two other reasons why the great world religions merit study. I call them *'justification from history'* and *'justification from culture'*.

(1) It is normal to insist on some understanding of biblical Judaism, Orthodox Christianity and the Protestant Reformation as prerequisites for a serious study of European history. If, then, one develops this historical perspective to take in the whole world, it clearly makes sense to study at least the great world religions. They have shaped the life of the nations and the interaction of nations, both peaceful and warlike. Without an appreciation of them, it would be nearly impossible to make sense of human history as a whole.

This *'justification from history'* applies equally to modern history: How can an intelligent person make sense of the Salman Rushdie affair without a minimum awareness of Islamic sensitivities regarding their prophet Muhammad? What this episode reveals is the power that religion has to produce a violent world. Part of the response of anybody who wishes to lessen the tension in many of the world's trouble spots is surely to get acquainted with the religious dimension of these quarrels. This applies to everyone, whether one be religious or non-religious. Here I should like to note how the new Junior Certificate Section A (*Communities of Faith*) invites pupils to look 'at some examples of conflict as a result of religious difference, in Ireland and elsewhere' (p. 12); and how the proposed Leaving Certificate Section C, 2.5c, wants pupils to study 'the role of religious belief in two recent conflict situations'.

(2) '*Justification from culture*' simply means that many of the world's cultural treasures have close links with the great world religions. A trip to Granada or Jerusalem will confirm this fact. Anyone with an interest in the aesthetic dimension of human experience could not fail to take into account the artistic, literary and musical contributions of the great world religions. It is not surprising, therefore, that Junior Certificate Section C invites pupils 'to examine the impact of [one major world] religion on its followers today and on other individuals and communities' (p. 20). The proposed Leaving Certificate Section C continues this approach. It includes the following 'understanding-objective': 'be aware that the major religious traditions ... continue to be of influence in the lives and cultures of their adherents'. This Section also proposes the following skill: 'recognise evidence of religious belief in contemporary culture'. In Section I (*Religion: The Irish Experience*), parts 2.2a and 2.2b study the archaeological and literary evidence for pre-Christian religion in Ireland.

While acknowledging many cultural gaps in the new syllabuses (for example, the link between religion and music is not mentioned), nevertheless, they both recognise in general terms that religious life can make a valuable contribution to human culture and human development.[16] On this basis alone, the material on the great world religions should be studied carefully, whenever possible, in Catholic schools of the future.

Conclusion

Teachers are divided among themselves as to the value, or even the possibility, of teaching the great world religions. Those who argue for, and those who argue against such teaching, have been allowed in this chapter to voice their opinions. On balance, my own conviction is that teaching the great world religions is both possible and valuable. Its possibility is lessened in practice by its inherent difficulties; but its value is probably to be found precisely in facing up to such challenges. In this chapter I also outline two general reasons for teaching the great world religions: in order to understand better and appreciate their impact on world history and on cultural life. I welcome the emphasis placed by the new syllabuses on the historical and cultural effects of the great world religions. I look forward to the time when serious-minded pupils in Irish second-level schools will be challenged by their educational encounter with Islam, Judaism, Buddhism and Hinduism.

Notes

1. See also P. M. Devitt, *ID*, pp. 111-112.
2. See M. Crawford and G. Rossiter, *TRSS*.
3. For a brief account of an Australian experiment in teaching Buddhism, see J. and J. Kondylas, 'Whyalla Cultural Exchange: Children's Experience with Buddhist Monks', in *CSS*, 70, no. 1 (May 1997), pp. 49-50. See also P. Murnane, 'Learning from the Buddha' in *The Tablet* (28 August 1999), pp. 60-61.
4. See B. Chatwin, *The Songlines*.
5. Published by Gill and Macmillan, Dublin, 1995.
6. See Aotearoa/New Zealand Catholic Bishops' Conference, *UF* series.
7. See B. V. Hill, 'Will and should the religious study appropriate to schools in a pluralist society foster religious relativism?' *BJRE*, 13 (1), 1990, pp. 126-136.
8. I refer to Islam here and in subsequent paragraphs by way of example only. One could just as easily refer to any other one of the great world religions. My argument would follow more or less the same lines.
9. See D. Lane, 'Afterword: The Expanding Horizons of Catholic Education', in P. Hogan and K. Williams (eds.), *FRIE*, p. 134.
10. See E. Hulmes, *Commitment and Neutrality in Religious Education*, pp. 29, 32.
11. This image has already been examined in Chapter 3 above.
12. See P. M. Devitt, *ID*, Chapter 8, 'Sharing faith with all people', which explores the dynamism of Christian faith in its relations with those who are non-Christian, post-Christian or even anti-Christian.
13. See D. Murray, *Secularism and the New Europe*, pp. 29, 42.
14. See D. J. Bosch, *Transforming Mission*, p. 375.
15. B. Griffith, *The Marriage of East and West*, p. 199.
16. For a broad treatment of this topic, see M. Grimmitt, *Religious Education and Human Development*.

Chapter 9

HOW TO TELL OUR BEST KEPT SECRET?

In the Appendix, when reflecting on *RDECS*, I shall examine one of that document's main assumptions, namely, that Catholic schools can be part of the Church's mission of evangelisation. The logic of this assumption can be represented as follows:

- The Church's main purpose is evangelisation (*a basic faith conviction*).
- Through providing a holistic education, the Catholic school plays a vital part in the drama of evangelisation (*a derivative faith conviction*).
- The work of justice is a constitutive part of evangelisation (*Catholic vision*).
- Therefore, Catholic schools ought to cultivate an atmosphere or ethos of simplicity and gospel poverty; ought to foster ecological awareness; and ought to encourage concern for the common good and international solidarity (*importance of school ethos*).
- Furthermore, all pupils in Catholic schools should be taught the Church's major social justice documents (*specific content*).[1]

In posing the question, 'How to tell our best kept secret?' I am asking, 'In the process of teaching the new Religious Education syllabuses, how can the social justice teaching of the Catholic Church be made accessible to pupils in schools today?' My answer is in six parts. Religion teachers of Catholic pupils ought to:

(1) Explain the new concepts (*specific content*).
(2) Connect these concepts to the *faith vision* that gives rise to them.
(3) Describe the living out of this vision, especially by Irish foreign missionaries *(Catholic vision in action)*.
(4) Contribute to the creation of a *just school ethos*.
(5) Relate justice to spirituality and worship.
(6) Appeal for courage and patience.

Specific content: Justice, Peace, and Integrity of Creation[2]

Writing more than a decade ago about the future of RE, Dermot Lane expressed the wish that 'basic themes like the preferential option for the poor, the struggle for justice, the defence of human rights, the equality and dignity of all persons, the creation of a better world, and concern for the development of the whole person would become part and parcel of religious education'.[3] His wish has been well fulfilled. All good religious education textbooks today deal in depth with these 'basic themes'.[4]

It comes as no surprise, therefore, to find that these justice themes are offered for study in the Junior Certificate RE syllabus. Section F (*The Moral Challenge*) in Part 4 (*Religious Morality in Action*) refers to 'justice, peace, life, stewardship, respect and integrity' (p. 42) as key concepts. The significance of these concepts had already been conveyed in the Introduction to the Junior Certificate syllabus, where it states that 'to promote ... equality for all' is one of the aims of Irish education. The proposed Leaving Certificate syllabus also tries to signal their importance by including a whole Section (F) on *Issues of Justice and Peace*. Both new RE syllabuses, therefore, clearly echo the spirit of the recently revised *General Directory for Catechesis*, which makes the following point: 'By means of catechesis, in which due emphasis is given to her social teaching, the Church desires to stir Christian hearts "to the cause of justice" and to a "preferential option or love for the poor", so that her presence may really be light that shines and salt that cures'.[5]

Most Religion teachers today are familiar with this new language of the faith. They are fluent in the idiom of social justice.[6] They are happy, when teaching Religion, to introduce to their pupils the idea of a 'preferential option'[7] for the poor. They even recognise a shared agenda between the Catholic Church and many of today's critical media thinkers. In teaching Religion from a justice perspective they often draw their justice content from the media. Furthermore, they alert their pupils to the possibility of an exciting, challenging and creative collaboration between the media and the Church, in the task of giving a shared 'preferential attentiveness to the voiceless'.[8] And this shared concern for the poor people of the modern world can also extend to a shared desire to foster the integrity of creation.[9] What used to be called 'development education'[10] is still a valid concern of most people today, even if the understanding of development has changed much in recent years. The proposed Leaving Certificate syllabus' exploration of 'The Religious Imperative to act for Justice and Peace in relation to the Environment' (Section F, 3) reflects very well this changed and richer understanding of development.

Faith vision

While it is good that these important social justice topics be at the heart of religious education, teachers need to go beyond this simple study of justice themes, to an examination of the 'kingdom vision' that gives life to the search for justice. Without vision, the people are dead. This point is well grasped by the authors of the Junior Certificate syllabus. On the one hand, they situate the topic of 'the poor' within the treatment of Jesus' preaching of the 'kingdom of God' (p. 17). In other words, they recognise how central concern for the poor must be for those who claim allegiance to Jesus and the 'kingdom of God' that he preached and witnessed to. On the other hand, the authors of the Junior Certificate syllabus know how to appeal to the incipient idealism of young adolescents; they explain religious vocation as a 'calling to serve' (p. 11) which is heard within one's community of faith, the normal location for challenging moral vision. The proposed Leaving Certificate syllabus tries to build on the justice foundations laid down for Junior Certificate pupils. This it does in a sub-section entitled 'Religious Perspectives on Justice and Peace' (F, 2.3). Here the Judaeo/Christian vision of justice is studied alongside similar themes from Islam, Hinduism and Buddhism. To situate the Catholic vision in this larger context of the other great world religions is never easy, because it requires of teachers and pupils that they recognise where the Catholic vision both compares with and contrasts to these other religious visions.

Nor is it easy to present the specific Catholic vision of social justice to pupils in school, for the elaboration of this vision within the Catholic Church has been a very long-drawn-out process. Even a cursory glance at the impressive list of recent Papal Encyclicals and Episcopal Letters with a social justice theme will reveal a complex learning process and an equally complex process of articulation of new insights.[11] One obvious example of a major *volte face* is the official attitude of the Catholic Church towards religious liberty, condemned by Pius IX in the nineteenth century, but championed now by John Paul II. Another example of a modern change in Catholic social teaching can be seen in the new *Catechism of the Catholic Church* (*CCC*). The *CCC* was first published in 1992, but since then the Catholic Church's teaching on capital punishment has been revised, and this revision has been incorporated into the official Latin edition published in 1997.[12] One is tempted to ask, in this regard, 'Is the Church still in her infancy with regard to her social teaching?' If one answers yes, then this is bound to affect the manner of teaching that one adopts in Religion class.

Catholic vision in action

In many parts of the Junior Certificate syllabus, an attempt is made to concretise the abstract concepts being studied. Thus Section B invites pupils to search 'for evidence of the impact ... on the lives of Christian believers today' (p. 17). And Section F is concerned precisely with 'religious morality in action' (p. 42), in other words, how one's religious moral vision affects the decision-making process that leads to moral action and moral living. The final phrase of the proposed Leaving Certificate Section F, 3g, refers to 'the teaching in action'.

This is a very helpful specification. It is good that pupils understand the content of the social justice teaching of their Church, and are also able to derive it theoretically from the central faith vision of Catholicism. But, unless they are introduced as well to the *people* who live this vision, there is a danger that their learning will be very abstract and unconnected with real life. It is only if one knows that the proclamation of social justice is matched by a living witness to social justice, that the real power of the teaching will be revealed. This is probably part of the reason why Fidel Castro, speaking as a committed Marxist, could comment so favourably on the present Pope's campaign for justice and civil rights.[13]

As Irish Catholics, we are very fortunate that we know so many of our country men and women, especially among our foreign missionaries, who have placed such a great emphasis on living justly themselves. We are fortunate too that many of them have also reflected on living justly in the light of faith, and have written numerous articles, books and even school texts on these issues.[14] Pupils learning Religion in Ireland today should be introduced over time to the writings of theologians such as Donal Dorr, on structural injustice,[15] and on down-to-earth spirituality and justice for women.[16]

In the context of the troubles in Northern Ireland, and the need for 'conflict resolution' (proposed Leaving Certificate syllabus, Section F, 2.4d), the pupils should be invited as well to consider the implications of what Niall O'Brien called a 'Revolution from the Heart'.[17] Through reflecting on provocative literature like this, and through learning the skills of 'social analysis' (proposed Leaving Certificate syllabus, Section F, 1), hopefully young Irish men and women will come to understand better why the Celtic Tiger doesn't always roar for everyone in Ireland today. They will understand why 'In Ireland we have, at the beginning of 1996, a thriving economy, yet "poverty, unemployment and exclusion will continue to be the core experience of a great many people's lives"'. [18]

Towards a just school ethos

It is clearly not enough for Religion teachers merely to talk about and explain the social justice imperative of the Catholic faith vision. If they are convinced of the role of school ethos in favouring this vision, then certain implications follow. The systematic research conducted by Patrick S. Fahy in Australian Catholic schools led him to conclude that 'students' social justice attitudes are best predicted by school climate and curriculum factors' rather than by the influence exerted on students by the home, or the peer group, or the school staff or even their own personality type.[19] One implication of this discovery is that Religion teachers need to be particularly attentive to the real ethos of their school, and constantly to assess this ethos in the light of the school's professed Christian vision.[20] In this context, it is important to recall what I said earlier in Chapter 1 about the 'social reconstruction' model of teaching. I pointed out there that any attempt at implementing such a teaching model would inevitably lead to a comparing of the underlying values of school ethos with the social justice content of Religion teaching.

Another related implication of Fahy's findings is that Religion teachers should invite their pupils to enter with them into this attentive mode. This could be described in religious terms as encouraging pupils' prophetic spirit, or in secular terms as pulling out their critical antennae. Neil Postman claims that the so-called 'hidden curriculum' of schools is not at all hidden, rather it is simply not attended to sufficiently.[21] Religion class, at its best, can be a key zone for learning skills of careful attentiveness. The overall effect of this attentive teaching and learning could be a help for pupils and staff in the process of 'devising structures' for 'a democratic culture'.[22] It could also benefit the Catholic Church at large, because more and more young people would thereby be empowered to pay closer attention to general 'Church life as massive latent curriculum'.[23]

Relating Justice to Worship
One of the greatest temptations in life is to opt for either-or, when life demands both-and. The same is often true of teaching Religion. One can so concentrate on justice issues as to neglect the worship aspect of Catholic faith. Or vice versa. The challenge today is not just to teach both justice and worship, but to teach both *in relation* to the other.[24] The work for justice needs the work of worship, or else burnout might occur. A living tree of worship demands a justice fruit, or else complacency might set in. To get the connection right between justice and worship is probably as difficult as trying to teach the wave theory of light in the context of the particle theory. But all the best thinkers insist that teachers must try to make the connection. 'Liturgy and justice have an intrinsic relationship to one another precisely because liturgy places us before the Just One to whom we say "Amen"'.[25] That is why, ideally, liturgy should help worshippers to 'develop a social conscience'.[26] That is also why 'solemnities are vain, words are empty, music a waste of time, prayer useless and rites nothing but lies, if they are not transformed by justice and mercy'.[27]

Courage and Patience needed
Gabriel Moran has written extensively on the need for the Church to be involved in 'social reform and social justice'.[28] But he always insists that justice cannot be forced into existence, no matter how hard

humans try. Ultimately, the coming of perfect justice is God's gift. Moran therefore encourages a certain attitude of hope and attentive waiting. David Hollenbach makes a similar point when he appeals for 'Courage and Patience: Education for Staying Power in the Pursuit of Peace and Justice'.[29] If Religion teachers are genuinely interested in teaching the justice demands of the Catholic faith, then they must cultivate in young people the courage and patience they will need if they are to survive in spite of failure. 'The practice of justice is ... no less than a new form of mysticism and holiness ... a political form of holiness'.[30] This new form of mysticism and holiness will probably require much soul-searching and a new asceticism.

Conclusion

Writing about the socio-political dimension of faith in *Immortal Diamond*, I suggested the following pen-picture of the modern believer: '*The believer has a serious responsibility, greater even than that of other human beings, effectively to work with all people of good will for the justice that leads to unity – and to do this in the light of the hoped for kingdom*'.[31] Now it is time to expand this pen-picture and to consider what a modern Religion teacher might be like. As a storyteller, the modern Religion teacher should tell 'our best kept secret', our story of a Just God, in a way that integrates all the six dimensions of justice identified in this chapter. Depending on the precise needs of the particular pupils, whether at Junior, Transition or Senior Cycle (for detailed knowledge of the concept of justice, for understanding of the origins of the social teaching of the Church, for concrete examples of just living, for the analytical skills to assess how just the school ethos really is, for the ability to connect justice to worship, for encouragement to work patiently for a more just world), any one of these six themes could be a main focus; but none should be omitted from the lively telling of the story.

Notes
1. See D. Dorr, *Option for the Poor;* and B.R. Hill, *Key Dimensions of Religious Education.* A very helpful analysis of the interplay between teaching justice and Liberation Theology can be found in D. S. Schipani, *Religious Education Encounters Liberation Theology.*
2. See D. Murray, *A Special Concern. The Philosophy of Education,* p. 21.
3. See D. A. Lane, 'The Challenge facing Religious Education today', in D. A. Lane (ed.), *REF,* p. 166.
4. For evidence of this claim, see P. M. Devitt, *ID,* pp. 106-108.
5. See Sacred Congregation of the Clergy, *GDC,* par. 17.
6. See H. Simian-Yofre, 'Justice', Chapter 7 in J. S. Marino (ed.), *BTRE.*
7. See M. Bezzina, 'Exercising a Preferential Option', in *CSS,* 69 (1), May 1996, pp. 31-34.
8. See D. Harrington, 'The Media and the Church', in D. A. Lane (ed.), *RCD,* p. 209.
9. R. C. Miller, 'Ecological Theology and Religious Education', in R. C. Miller (ed.), *TRE,* p. 358.
10. See B. Davies, 'Development Education in the Secondary School', in D. O'Leary (ed.), *REYA.*
11. See *Rerum Novarum* (Leo XIII, 1891), *Quadragesimo Anno* (Pius XI, 1931), *Mater et Magistra* (John XXIII, 1961), *Pacem in Terris* (John XXIII, 1963), *Gaudium et Spes* (Vatican II, 1965), *Populorum Progressio* (Paul VI, 1967), *Justice in the World* (Synod of Bishops, 1971), *Octagesima Adveniens* (Paul VI, 1971), *Evangelii Nuntiandi* (Paul VI, 1975), *The Work of Justice* (Irish Bishops, 1977), *Laborem Exercens* (John Paul II, 1981), *Sollicitudo Rei Socialis* (John Paul II, 1987), *Centesimus Annus* (John Paul II, 1991), *Tertio Millennio Adveniente* (John Paul II, 1994), *The Common Good* (Bishops of England and Wales, 1996), *Prosperity with a Purpose: Christian Faith and Values in a Time of Rapid Economic Growth* (Irish Catholic Bishops' Conference, 1999).
12. John Paul II, *CCC,* par. 2267.

13. See F. McDonagh, 'The Curtain rises in Havana', *The Tablet*, (24 January 1998), p. 101.

14. See T. Larkin and P. McAndrew, *The GATEWAY series: A Mission, Justice and Development Manual for Religious Educators.* See also M. Hanly, *Ireland's Link with the Global Refugee Crisis.*

15. See D. Dorr, *Spirituality and Justice*, Chapter 4.

16. See D. Dorr, *Integral Spirituality.*

17. See N. O'Brien, *Revolution from the Heart.*

18. C. Dorgan, 'Foolish Dream or Hope for the Future?', quoting from CORI's Justice Office in S. Mac Réamoinn (ed.), *The Church in a New Ireland*, p. 58.

19. P. S. Fahy, *FCC*, p. 139.

20. See P. O'Hare (ed.), *Education for Peace and Justice*, especially the chapters by T. Groome, 'Religious Education for Justice by Educating Justly'; by M.C. Boys, 'A Word about Teaching Justly'; and by P. O'Hare, 'The Renewal of Education and the nurturing of Justice and Peace.'

21. N. Postman, *TACA*, p. 51.

22. See E. G. Cassidy, 'Religion and Culture: The Freedom to be an Individual,' in E. G. Cassidy (ed.), *FCIC*, p. 63.

23. See E. D. Gray, 'Feminist Theology and Religious Education', in R. C. Miller (ed.), *TRE*, p. 222.

24. See T. Balasuriya, *Eucharist and Human Liberation.*

25. K. Hughes, 'Liturgy, Justice and Peace', in P. O'Hare (ed.), *EPJ*, p. 199.

26. J. D. Crichton, *The Once and Future Liturgy*, p. 103.

27. J. Gelineau, *The Liturgy Today and Tomorrow*, pp. 122-3.

28. G. Moran, 'Social Reform: On the way to Justice', in P. O'Hare, (ed.), *EPJ*, p. 38.

29. See P. O'Hare (ed.), *ibid.*

30. D. Harrington, *What is Morality?*, p. 196.

31. P. M. Devitt, *ID*, p. 63.

Chapter 10

WHY DID GOD MAKE US MALE AND FEMALE?

In each of the chapters so far, my foundational question, *'How can the NCCA RE syllabuses be integrated into the catechetical work of teaching Religion to Catholic pupils in Irish schools today?'* has led on to a more specific question dealing with some aspect of Religion teaching.

In this chapter, however, the question posed is one of a different order. Although it derives from the fact that the proposed Leaving Certificate syllabus has a section entitled *Women, Religion and the Christian tradition*, it is, strictly speaking, a question that transcends the work of Irish schools, and has an importance for the entire life of the Catholic Church. I hope to show how it might also have some impact on the teaching of Religion to Catholic pupils.

Blurred vision

According to St John's Gospel, the Word of God was made flesh in a man, Jesus of Nazareth. But, what if the Word had been made flesh in a woman? In principle, this could have happened. God, being 'neither man nor woman, transcends the human distinction between the sexes'.[1] This means that *both* men and women can, and really do, image God. What is more, the mystical body of Christ (one traditional way of describing the Church) is made flesh each day now in *both* men and women.

The two healing sacraments of the Church (Reconciliation and Anointing) are celebrated by *both* men and women. Marriage is jointly celebrated by a woman *and* a man. The Catholic tradition ordains only male human beings, and this means that presidency at the Eucharist and ministration of most sacraments is still reserved for men. However, in terms of fundamental Christian identity (established in Baptism, Confirmation and Eucharist), one's sex matters not at all. What matters is faith, hope and love. Mary, virgin and mother, is uniquely holy and model of holiness for *both* men and women.[2] This insight surely needs to be emphasised in the Church today. Is there a hint of it in the proposed Leaving Certificate syllabus, Section E (*Women, Religion and the Christian Tradition*) where part 2.3 includes 'new interpretations and understanding of the role and significance of Mary'?

Religious life is for *both* men and women, the majority being women. Religion teaching is done by *both* men and women, the majority being women. However, while theological teaching is done by *both* men and women, the majority are still men. Liturgy is celebrated by *both* men and women, the vast majority being women. Administration in the Church is open to *both* men and women, the vast majority being men.[3] The service of the needy is provided by *both* men and women; there is no known majority. The canonised saints of the Catholic Church are *both* men and women, the vast majority being men. In the General Liturgical Calendar (taking no account of feasts of Our Lord, Our Lady, the Holy Innocents, All Saints and the angels, and counting groups of saints as one), there are 140 men saints and only 27 women saints: there are five men saints for every woman saint. Given these facts, and given also the impact of recent feminist writings, it should come as no surprise that there is a section in the proposed Leaving Certificate syllabus on women but no corresponding section on men.

This analysis of the sacramental, social, celebrational and organisational life of the Church today reveals that the process of enfleshment of the Body of Christ is quite uneven. It is a fair question to ask, 'why is this so?' Maybe sin has something to do with this, since sin is a kind of distorted vision. Because all humans are sinners, they see and interpret things other than the way God sees them and interprets them. Sin is blurred vision. It can cause people to miss the mark and lose their way. Maybe that is why, in the Church, the enfleshment of God's Son is recognised and emphasised more in men than in women.

The Church and women

Increasingly today women are asking, 'Why must the Church be like this?' They are assuming a prophetic stance. The prophet is God's spokesperson, and tries to interpret life in terms of God's perspective.

Women today assume that their interpretation of life is valid and should be listened to. However, since women have until now seldom preached the Gospel, it follows that 'the fullness of human reflection has not yet been acknowledged by the Christian community'.[4] The four evangelists were men, and so too have been all the official, apostolic teachers of the Church from day one. This means that normal male bias and normal, limited male insights have shaped our Christian traditional wisdom. This, I suggest, is bad, not just for men and for women, but even for the full truth of the Gospel itself. Katherine Zappone laments the paucity of women-voices in the Church and notes that 'female experience of relatedness with the deity did not funnel into the construction of religious symbols'.[5] We are all the poorer for this.

Writing about the great contribution made to Ireland and to Irish Catholicism by Nano Nagle, Catherine McAuley, Mary Aikenhead and Teresa Ball, one theologian-bishop states that 'a Church in which women were passive and/or resentful would be failing to show the full truth of the Gospel'.[6] In an earlier chapter, I pointed out the ongoing need for inculturation of the faith. Because Christian faith needs to be inculturated afresh in contact with every new culture, because each human culture must be helped to find its proper faith-voice, it follows that the woman-half of human culture and of Church culture needs to find its voices too.[7] If it is so important for Ireland that we 'Irish' the faith, it is equally important for everybody that we 'woman' the faith. Because women have been silent for too long, the Church has been deprived of a vital articulation of the truth. There is a pressing need today for women to speak with courage out of this long silence. In this task they will find support from the efforts of some men who have themselves also been wrapped in silence. The paradox of silence as a source of truth is well captured in these words: 'His voice emerged from silence and testified to what in silence was revealed as real, to life'.[8]

Competing voices

Not everybody believes that this is possible or even worthwhile. According to some feminists, such as Mary Daly, the Church is so anti-woman that it merits no further consideration. It should be abandoned forthwith by any sane person, especially by any self-respecting woman. Even less critical feminists have many serious problems with the Church's treatment of women. Marina Warner, for example, laments the manner in which devotion to the Blessed Virgin Mary within the Church has been allowed to develop in ways that demean the average woman: 'The priesthood is closed to women because they are considered a secondary image of the maker, too gentle and timid by nature, and destined to serve either their husbands and children as wives and mothers or priests and children as nuns'.[9] Anne Thurston finds it ironic that the traditional role of women as providers of nourishment and as table-hosts should be judged by the Catholic Church to be in no way relevant to Eucharistic presidency.[10]

While recognising that the Church has often been guilty of the sin of sexism, other feminists are more hopeful for the future and more confident that the Church can be transformed. 'It is not "forgive and forget", as if nothing wrong had ever happened, but "forgive and go forward", building on the mistakes of the past and the energy generated by reconciliation to create a new future'.[11] Elizabeth Johnston, in her masterly elaboration of a theology of the 'communion of saints', shows clearly how a recovery of the lost voices of women can help the Church to recover its inner meaning as communion of faithful friends of God, wherein everybody is called to an equal share in the inner holiness of the creative and saving God of Jesus Christ, and can challenge all members of the Church to ask why this theological equality is not represented more clearly in the social and political life of the Church.[12]

A return to source

I have noted an uneven enfleshment of men and women in the Church, and I have also examined a range of modern reflections on this fact. Now is the time to make a brief return to the source of our faith-vision, and to pose the basic question, 'Why did God make us male and female?' The Book of Genesis did not ask this precise question but, by examining some of its authors' assumptions, we may be able to suggest an answer for today.

Pupils who carefully study the proposed Leaving Certificate RE syllabus should be well able to make sense of these assumptions. In

Section F (*Issues of Justice and Peace*), part 3c, pupils will study 'the creation texts in Genesis and the concepts of stewardship and domination'. While Section H on The Bible does not specify a study of Genesis 1 and 2, its exploration of 'biblical interpretation today' (part 1.2d) and its 'exploration and analysis ... of the text as a sacred text' (part 4) should enable pupils to transcend a purely literal reading of these important Genesis texts, and understand their underlying theological and anthropological assumptions. It is also worth noting that Section J (*Religion and Science*) explores 'the Judaeo Christian understanding of creation' (part 2.4c) and, in the context of the modern debate about origins, treats of 'Hebrew stories of creation' (part 3.1c).

Genesis claims that all men and women are created '*in the image of God*'. Then it says that all humans should '*have dominion over the fish*', etc. Clearly men and women, working together in care of God's earth, are meant to image or reflect God's creative lordship ('dominion') over the whole earth. There is no suggestion here that humans should destroy, damage or pollute the earth. Rather, women and men should collaborate together, in care of the earth, which is truly God's 'very good' creation.[13]

Now that geneticists have shown how interrelated all life forms are, it is interesting to recall the assumption of Genesis that humans are made '*from the dust of the ground*'. Human beings share the same atomic elements as all the material in the universe; human beings share about 98 per cent of their genetic make-up with chimpanzees. However, humans are very special, since God has breathed into human '*nostrils the breath of life*'. This means that humans are earthly spirits or, perhaps, spiritual earthlings.[14]

The divine spirit/breath in human life effectively transforms every dimension of human existence. In the context of human sexuality, the divine spirit/breath so suffuses the man and the woman that their coming together (which is inevitably sexual, though not necessarily genital) is an image, albeit faint, of the very divine community. Human beings, as sexual beings, as hints of God on earth, are meant to share life with each other. By becoming companions, by sharing deeply in one another's lives, women and men are 'healing ... the divisions so evident in our society'.[15]

In God's plan, '*it is not good that the man should be alone; I will make him a helper as his partner*'. To interpret this word 'helper' to mean that women are naturally subordinate to men, is a strong temptation that people have often given in to. However, scholars have noted that this word 'helper' elsewhere in the scriptures describes a divine characteristic, God's saving relationship with the entire human race. So, according to Genesis, woman is to man as God is to humanity: a saving presence. Once again, the special quality of human genital sex is being hinted at here. At one level, it is a partnership of mutual support, in which woman and man are of equal dignity: '*the rib that the Lord God had taken from the man he made into a woman*'. But, at an even deeper level, hidden at the heart of that mutuality, there is a roaring divine fire that heals, saves and binds more closely.

Being made in the image of a creative God means that, when men and woman marry, when '*they become one flesh*', they are not just company for one another or equal sexual partners, but also potentially pro-creators of children. In creating them '*male and female*' and in inviting them to '*be fruitful and multiply*', God laid a further creative burden on human shoulders, that of generating a new community or family.

So, 'Why did God make us male and female?' For stewardship of the earth, for company, for sex, for making children. All of these are possible answers. I should like now to suggest another answer. My answer begins by recognising that the entire universe already shouts out the beauty of God; and it continues by rejoicing that the chimpanzee screeches out the praise of God's grace. My answer realises that the cosmos and its animals are indeed powerful echoes and wonderful images of the creator and provider God. But my answer wants even more. I should like to suggest now that God made us male and female in order that we might have in our daily sight an even more beautiful image of God, and in our ears an even crisper echo of God: men and women *together* reveal God best.

Naming other outstanding women (and men)
While warmly welcoming Section E of the proposed Leaving Certificate syllabus, and all it attempts to achieve in the context of sexism and feminism, I must now ask, 'What more is needed for

Catholic school RE?' Since this Section on *Women, Religion and the Christian Tradition* is not obligatory, nobody knows how many pupils will study it. Now, the only obligatory Section in the entire Leaving Certificate syllabus is *The Search for Meaning and Values*. Therefore, if the generality of pupils are to benefit from listening to women-voices, it is imperative that women's role in this search for meaning and values be recognised and studied. The outstanding women thinkers, novelists, painters, musicians, poets, philosophers, scientists and theologians should figure here. They should figure, first of all, because of their excellence; and, secondly, to balance the usual tendency towards mentioning only men.

In Section G of the proposed Leaving Certificate syllabus, the women mystics (Teresa of Avila, Julian of Norwich, Catherine of Siena) are studied only by honours students. I recommend that somehow these names would at least be mentioned in the course studied by general pupils. They deserve to be known, not just because they were great women, but also because of the excellence of their lives and the power of their writings. They should have a place of honour in any study of the Christian life.

In recommending the mentioning of more women's names in the new syllabuses, I also recommend the mentioning of more men's names too. In fact, a close study of both syllabuses will reveal that very few men are mentioned in either. This probably flows from the fact that the syllabus is ideas-driven. I agree with Neil Postman that school, in general, should be 'ideas-driven'.[16] However, since religion is about people much more than ideas, there will be a need in religious education always to show how concrete people actually manage to enflesh their religious ideas in daily living. This is what lies behind the *Catholic* veneration and celebration of the saints. I have already alluded to this issue in the chapter entitled, 'Why teach Church history?'

In the context of giving ear to the voice of women, it is also important not to silence the voices of men. Even St Paul, whom many criticise for his anti-women stance, often drew upon womanly images to talk about his own faith and his own mission. 'But we were gentle among you, like a nurse tenderly caring for her own children. So deeply do we care for you that we are determined to share with you not only the gospel of God but also our very selves, because you have become very dear to us' (1 Thess 2: 7-8). Here is a side of St Paul that needs to be recovered and celebrated.

Naming prophetic women
The failure of the proposed Leaving Certificate syllabus to mention any outstanding women thinkers is serious enough. So too is its limited treatment of women mystics. But a far more serious lacuna, in the overall context of religious education, is *religion*'s own failure to advert to women's role in the prophetic ministry. Prophets are those who speak on behalf of God, because they have been inspired by God's vision. Christian prophets see the world through the eyes of Christ, judging its good and bad points only from his perspective. However, we know the names of very few women prophets from the Hebrew scriptures or from the New Testament. And yet, when one recognises the meaning of prophecy, as vision and critique, it is hard to imagine they did not exist.[17] Do women have no vision? Do women never critique? Do women never energise the Church?[18]

Let us take a moment now to examine the ancient tradition of venerating and canonising saints. When we reflect on many of the women saints, we are immediately confronted by their prophetic quality. They simply refuse to be bound by culture, either secular or religious. Many women saints transcend the cultural expectations of their day, in which a good woman was married, had children, and obeyed her husband.

There is a difficulty today in talking meaningfully about saints. The exaggerations of the hagiographers and the traditional legacy of 'plaster saints' can easily prevent us from imagining real, flesh and blood, living saints. In an otherwise excellent tribute to his recently deceased sister, Princess Diana, Earl Spencer seems to assume that saintliness is unreal and unconnected with being human.[19] These are some of his words:

> There is a temptation to rush, to canonise your memory. There is no need to do so. You stand *tall enough as a human being* of unique qualities, and do not need to be seen as a *saint*.

Indeed, to sanctify your memory would be *to miss out on the very core of your being* - your wonderfully mischievous sense of humour with a laugh that bent you double, your joy for life transmitted wherever you took your smile and the sparkle in those unforgettable eyes, your boundless energy which you could barely contain *(italics mine)*.

I do not wish here to discuss whether or not Diana was a saint. Rather, I wish to challenge the *idea* of saintliness implicit in the earl's stunning speech. I do not share the assumptions contained in the italicised phrases. Saintliness is not something added to one's *humanity*; rather, it is the divine spark glowing in a human life, and setting it on fire with love. Saintliness can never miss out on the very *core* of one's being. In fact, it is precisely there that holiness grows, because it is there that love grows. And saints are not canonised for their own sakes, but rather for the sake of the rest of us, who are still living, to inspire and challenge us to deeper love.

The stories of selected women saints[20]
The following is a small selection of women saints of note. It merits consideration as possible additional content for Catholic pupils. It would also provide good material with which to attempt to answer these questions, 'What kinds of people have been proposed as saints?' and 'What understanding of sainthood has led to their acceptance as saints?'

Cecilia (2-3 century): Virgin and Martyr (22 November)
As early as the fourth century, Cecilia was already celebrated as one of the greatest Roman martyrs. Her name is in the first Eucharistic Prayer (the Roman Canon). A basilica was erected in Trastevere, Rome, in her honour in the fifth century. The *Passion of Saint Cecilia* presented her as a perfect example of Christian womanhood, who preserved her virginity and suffered martyrdom for the love of Christ. Tradition names her the patron saint of musicians.

Monica (332-87): Mother of St Augustine (27 August)
Born in Carthage, North Africa, of a Christian family, Monica was married while still young to a pagan, Patricius. Augustine was the elder

of her three children. Under the influence of his father, Augustine grew indifferent to the faith and drifted from the practice of virtue. Through patience and gentleness, she converted her husband. She also prayed unceasingly to God for Augustine's conversion, and her prayers were answered, shortly before she died. While waiting to return home with Augustine and his brother, she died of a fever at Ostia (the port of Rome). She was immortalised in Augustine's great book, the *Confessions*. Her dying words were (as she lay, far from her native land): 'Lay this body wherever it may be. Let no care of it disturb you; this only I ask of you, that you should remember me at the altar of the Lord wherever you may be'.

Scholastica (480-543): Virgin (10 February)
Scholastica was the sister of St Benedict, the father of Western Monasticism. She became a nun (the first Benedictine nun) and lived under her brother's direction near Monte Cassino. Tradition has it that Benedict saw her soul ascend to heaven in the form of a dove. Paintings often show her with crosier and crucifix or with a dove flying from her mouth.

Margaret of Scotland (1045-93): Queen and mother (16 November)
Margaret was the granddaughter of King Edmund Ironside of England and great niece of St Stephen of Hungary. Margaret was born in Hungary, where her father was in exile. She was given in marriage to Malcolm III, king of the Scots, with whom she had six sons and two daughters. An outstanding mother and queen, she was also founder of the Benedictine Abbey of Dunfermline, where she is buried. Margaret is remembered for her promotion of justice and her great love of the poor. She was canonised in 1251.

Clare of Assisi (1194-1253): Virgin (11 August)
Clare was irresistibly drawn by Francis' ideal of Christian poverty, and at the age of eighteen, ran away from home and took the veil from Francis himself, who also provided her with refuge among the Benedictine nuns. She was founder and ruler of an order of nuns (Poor Clares) at San Damiano. Popes, cardinals and bishops came there to

consult her. She led a very austere life, abounding in works of piety and charity. Possibly as influential as Francis himself in the rapid spreading of the Franciscan movement, Clare was canonised two years after her death. In art, she is usually represented with a monstrance in her hand.

Catherine and Teresa

When the commentary on Section G (*Worship, Prayer and Ritual*) is published, I feel sure it will offer some detailed information regarding Catherine of Siena (1347-80): Virgin, Doctor of the Church (29 April); and Teresa of Avila (1515-82): Virgin, Doctor of the Church (15 October).

Thérèse of Lisieux (1873-97): Virgin, Doctor of The Church (1 October)

Also known as Teresa of the Child Jesus or The Little Flower, she was born at Alençon in France. She entered the Carmelite monastery at Lisieux and practised the virtues of humility, gospel simplicity and confidence in God. She was appointed novice-mistress at the age of twenty-two. Her autobiography, *Story of a Soul*, reveals her inner struggles to believe and contains the remarkable sentence, 'I've found my vocation, and my vocation is love'. She was canonised in 1925. Given her youth, her relatively sheltered convent life and her limited academic background, she was, paradoxically, declared patron saint of the foreign missions (along with St Francis Xavier) and, more recently, Doctor of the Church.

Other important women

As well as being introduced to this 'great cloud of witnesses' (Heb 12:1), Catholic pupils should also be told the stories of other great prophetic women (both Christian and non-Christian). The list is endless. It could include Brigid, Nano Nagle, Mary Wollstonecraft,[21] Edel Quinn, Simone Weil,[22] Sister Stanislaus, Mother Teresa of Calcutta, Mama Tina of Ho Chi Minh city and many others. One of my own favourites is Antigone. I mention Antigone because, through her humanity and her loving care for her dead brother, she challenged the entire panoply of political might in ancient Greece. Not only did she capture the imagination of the ancient Greeks but, in the context of World War II, she once again captured the imagination of an oppressed nation, the people of France.[23] A truly prophetic woman, and well worth listening to.

Conclusion

The proposed Leaving Certificate syllabus Section entitled *Women, Religion and the Christian Tradition* has challenged me to reflect on the place of women in the life of the Church. It has also provoked some critical assessment of the strengths and weaknesses of this Section for teaching Religion to Catholic pupils. The many suggestions I have made have one thing in common: people are central to the Church, and people's voices need to be listened to with greater care.[24] In particular, I have called for the naming of great women thinkers, artists and mystics, and for study of their insights by pupils in school. I have also suggested that many of the great women saints were *prophetic* figures, whose lives need to be remembered and whose stories need to be retold.

Furthermore, I would like to suggest that the Section on *Women, Religion and the Christian Tradition* is of such inherent importance for every member of the Catholic Church, that it should be taught to *both* boys and girls (if possible, together in class); and that *both* men and women should be asked to teach it.

Notes

1. John Paul II, *CCC*, par. 239.
2. The following are some recent articles dealing with Mary and related themes: M. T. Malone, 'Mary Mother of God: An Educational Problem?' *BJRE*, 12 (1) 1989; C. Mangan, 'Mary and Women,' in J. Hyland (ed.), *MIC*; L. O'Reilly, 'Mary, the woman not the girl', *The Furrow* (October 1992); D. Flanagan, 'Mary and the unremembered past', *DL* (May/June 1993); M. Ryan, 'Meeting the Blessed Virgin Mary', *CSS*, 67 (2) October 1994; and C. Renehan, 'Preaching on Mary', *The Furrow*, (December 1996).
3. See A. Miller, 'Women in the Vatican', *The Tablet*, (29 March/5 April 1997).
4. See C. C. Murphy, *An Introduction to Christian Feminism*, p. 101.
5. K. Zappone, *The Hope for Wholeness: A Spirituality for Feminists*, p. 29.
6. D. Murray, *The Future of the Faith*, p. 18.
7. The difficulty experienced by one woman in finding her authentic 'voice' is well documented by M. Cardinal, *The Words to Say it*. For a powerful study of the position of women in Irish society today, and of their struggle to find their voices, see P. O'Connor, *Emerging Voices: Women in Contemporary Irish Society*.
8. T. Del Prete, *Thomas Merton and the Education of the Whole Person*, p. 97.
9. M. Warner, *Alone of All her Sex*, p. 191.
10. See A. Thurston, *Because of her Testimony: The Word in Female Experience*. See also E. McDonagh, who echoes these sentiments in 'Fruit of the Earth – work of human hands', in M. Grey, A. Heaton and D. Sullivan (eds.), *The Candles are Still Burning*, p. 28.
11. C. Osiek, *Beyond Anger: On Being a Feminist in the Church*, pp. 65, 76. For reflections on feminism and sexism from the perspective of religious education, see M. Harris and G. Moran, 'Feminism and the Imagery of RE', *BJRE*, 12 (1) 1989; and C. Hallows, 'Sexism and RE in Roman Catholic Schools', *BJRE*, 12 (1) 1989.
12. See E. Johnston, *Friends of God and Prophets*.

13. For a good introduction to the topic, Creation in Scripture and Tradition, see S. McDonagh, *The Greening of the Church*, especially Part 2.

14. Groome maintains that we humans have 'a homing instinct for God.' See T. Groome, *EFL*, p. 79.

15. See M. Harris, 'Isms and Religious Education,' in G. Durka and J. Smith, *Emerging Issues in Religious Education*, p. 52.

16. See N. Postman, *Teaching as a Conserving Activity*, p. 125.

17. For an examination of the role of prophecy within the life of Christian faith, see P. M. Devitt, *ID*, Chapter 3, 'Looking at Life Through the Eyes of Christ'.

18. This idea comes from W. Brueggemann, *The Prophetic Imagination*, p. 14.

19. For the full text of this speech, see *The Irish Times*, 8 September, 1997, p. 8.

20. A helpful resource for these stories is *The Book of Saints*, compiled by the Benedictine monks.

21. See S. McGrath, 'Mary Wollstonecraft – the Educator', *CSS*, 65 (2) October 1992.

22. M. Muggeridge, writing in the Foreword to S. Weil, *Gateway to God*, likens Simone to Mother Teresa: 'They are both pilgrims of the absolute – Simone of absolute truth, and Mother Teresa of absolute love; the two, of course, amounting to the same thing' (p. 10).

23. See J. Anouilh, *Antigone*.

24. For a powerful example of modern Dublin people being given a chance to voice their faith, see B. Flanagan, *The Spirit of the City: Voices from Dublin's Liberties*.

APPENDIX

The Religious Dimension of Education in a Catholic School

Anybody teaching in a Catholic school today, either as a Religion teacher or a teacher of a secular subject, will be enriched by a careful reading of *The Religious Dimension of Education in a Catholic School (RDECS)*. Published in 1988 by the Congregation for Catholic Education in Rome, this document is one of the latest in a series of fine educational reflections offered by the Vatican to the world of Catholic education.[1] It is a vision document, painting an ideal for Catholic schools to aim at in today's world and encouraging them to take stock of how well they are approaching the ideal.[2] The document is important for many reasons, not the least of which is the large number of Catholic schools world-wide. In 1985 'there were 151,126 Catholic schools with 38,243,304 students'.[3]

The Structure of RDECS

A short introduction outlines the purpose of the document, which is to ask whether or not the educational suggestions of the Council Fathers have been put into practice (2). Then follows an invitation to school authorities to study the general guidelines and adapt them within their own local contexts (5). The main body of the document contains five sections, which deal in turn with the religious dimension of:
- Young people in a changing world
- The school climate
- Intellectual work and the general school curriculum
- Religious Instruction and formation
- The process of evaluating educational goals.

Much consultation preceded the writing of this document. The wisdom of many practitioners has been distilled into a dense text. It should be read slowly, and with great care. It is like a brandy to be sipped, rather than a wine to be quaffed.

Integration of faith and culture

The key theme of *RDECS* is the integration of faith, culture and life. Faith and culture can be so identified with one another as to be confused with each other. Examples of this would be easy to find in Europe during the Middle Ages or in countries such as Iran today. In each of these cases, the enrichment of the local culture through being permeated by Christian or Islamic values is plain for all to see. Less plain, but no less real, is the difficulty for infidels (unbelievers) or outsiders to be accepted as part of such a world. In an effort to improve matters, many peoples have opted to try to separate faith and culture, to put religion and life in separate compartments. While there are obvious advantages here, especially for minorities in a given country, there are problems too. It is hard to be a person of faith in one compartment of one's life and a person of culture in another. People naturally want to be integrated in life.

RDECS proposes a different way of conceptualising the relationship between faith and culture. While faith is 'not to be identified with any culture', it should, however, 'inspire every culture' (53). This means that faith will have different shapes or forms or tones in different cultures. It will inspire people from within the culture, being pro-culture wherever it finds the good and the true and the beautiful, but being counter-cultural whenever it finds contrary values incarnated in culture. This perspective is also that of Michael Paul Gallagher, who asks 'how faith-choices can be made both within and against a culture'.[4] While Gallagher allows that 'post-modernity can certainly be more friend than foe for religious commitment today',[5] he also appeals for 'cultural discernment', by which he means 'acknowledging that there are authentic values within the culture which need liberating from the deceptions'.[6]

This approach to the faith-culture conversation is very reminiscent of what Neil Postman calls a 'thermostatic view' of the education-culture dialogue. According to this view, 'the major role of education in the years immediately ahead is to help conserve that which is both necessary to a human survival and threatened by a furious and exhausting culture'.[7] The main aim of education, according to Postman, is to offer 'a program for subverting the prevailing biases of the culture'.[8] Nano Brennan echoes this sentiment when she describes

Christian education as 'a process of inculturation and contestation'.[9] A similar viewpoint is expressed very forcefully by an emeritus professor of English Literature, who argues that Catholic schools must be preserved in Scotland for the sake of the nation's soul: 'Catholic education is a kind of spiritual environmentalism, a defence against a contamination of the spirit'.[10]

The two new Religious Education syllabuses have many significant references to the faith-culture dialogue, e.g., Junior Certificate Section B deals with the 'context' of Jesus of Nazareth (p. 15); Section C examines the 'cultural context' of the great world religions (p. 21); Section D considers the beginnings of faith 'especially in youth culture' (p. 28), and also 'the variety of world views in today's culture' (p. 31) – by this variety it means 'atheism, agnosticism, secularism, materialism, and fundamentalism'. The dialogue between faith and culture also figures in the proposed Leaving Certificate Section A, 4.2b, which deals with 'ways in which religions relate to this secular culture'; Section B, 1.2, entitled 'Jesus and his message in contemporary culture'; Section E, 3, where Christian women are studied under the heading 'contribution to cultural context/religious tradition'; and Section I, 3.1b, which explores 'the 'inculturation' of Christianity in Ireland'. Here is material for study which *RDECS* would clearly welcome in every Catholic school.

RDECS recognises that in today's world there is often a wide gap or chasm between the Gospel and culture (15). In such a schizophrenic world, what can the Catholic school achieve? It can help pupils by 'mediating between faith and culture' (31), or by bringing 'faith, culture and life into harmony' (34). The Catholic school achieves its educational goals by 'blending human culture with the message of salvation into a co-ordinated programme' (100). It offers pupils a rounded educational experience 'that integrates the human and the Christian' (102). What is being described here is clearly the ideal Catholic school, 'able to bring the light of Christ into every aspect of school life'.[11] Such a Catholic school is 'holistic' rather than 'dualistic'. It realises instinctively that 'God's creative action is to be found in mathematics, geography, science, literature, history, art and music as well as in Religious Education classes. When the two worlds become totally separate, the message of Christ is betrayed'.[12]

In practical terms, this means that the whole school curriculum is to be taught in such a way that pupils gradually recognise the close and intimate links between faith and human culture. Pupils should slowly begin to sense that 'the world of human culture and the world of religion are not like two parallel lines that never meet' (51). Pupils in second-level schools are exposed every day to the challenging questions that human culture asks of faith, and so they need help 'to attain that synthesis of faith and culture which is necessary for faith to be mature' (52).

Therefore, a major objective in the teaching of positive science would be to help pupils to appreciate the resonance between faith and science (54). *RDECS* encourages teachers of biology to work out of a holistic understanding of the human person, which would not abstract from but rather include the religious dimension (55). Those Religion teachers who elect to teach the new syllabuses will find many helpful resources for performing such tasks, especially in Junior Certificate Section D, one of whose objectives is that pupils should 'be able to identify points of conflict and points of contact between the scientific and religious world views of creation' (p. 31); and also in the proposed Leaving Certificate Section J, 2.4, which deals with the topic 'Science and Religion in Dialogue'.

As pupils get older and develop their thinking skills, it is crucial that they learn how to make sense of human culture in the light of faith (52). They can be assisted here by the teaching of history, because history depends on a critical examination of texts (58). There is also a way of teaching geography that allows for a critical evaluation of the human use and abuse of the natural world, and alerts pupils to the major environmental challenges and the key issues of social injustice.[13]

The role of the humanities, especially literature and the arts, is also highlighted. Here pupils can be helped to deepen their aesthetic sensitivity and to discover that 'in every human culture, art and literature have been closely linked to religious beliefs'(60).[14] Eoin Cassidy claims 'that the aesthetic dimension of experience will never lose its power to evoke an awareness of the spiritual'.[15] And that is why a true Catholic school will always be characterised by a vibrant debate between culture and the Gospel (57).[16] For such a debate to flourish, the entire teaching staff would need to be united in the pursuit of this common objective (99).

In the proposed Leaving Certificate syllabus, Section H, 3, is entitled 'The Literature of the Bible'. The study of narrative, parable, symbol, myth and poetry in the Bible can clearly be helped by the parallel study of modern secular literature. What has been said about poetry in general is also true in regard to much religious language: 'a poem is a performance in language in which at every point things are happening simultaneously. Hence the notorious resistance to paraphrase with which poems scandalously affront mere intellect'.[17]

Evangelisation and maturity of faith

RDECS makes a strong case for the Catholic school as an agent of evangelisation 'not through complementary or parallel or extra-curricular activity, but of its very nature: its work of educating the Christian person' (33). The Catholic school, through the holistic education just now described above, plays a vital part in the drama of the Church's evangelising mission (101). It is not just the Religion class but the entire Catholic school that contributes to this mission (69). Though the Catholic school is not the only agent of evangelisation, it is indeed a major component in the evangelisation of Catholic young people today (66).

All of this is asserted, in spite of the fact that not all pupils and not all staff of Catholic schools may be Catholics. This may indeed make evangelisation difficult, but it certainly does not mean that evangelisation should be curtailed. The very least that can be done for non-Catholics or non-believers in Catholic schools is to help them to discover within their own experience a religious sense of life (108). Kevin Williams has well stated that 'if the children of non-believing parents are not exposed to religion in school, they may never encounter religion as a significant source of meaning in human life'.[18] Every such exposure to and encounter with religion should take place with due regard to people's freedom. To evangelise means to offer but never to impose the Good News (6).

Since the preaching of the Gospel has, as a constitutive part, the work for justice, it makes sense to put before pupils in Catholic schools some of the riches of Catholic social teaching. Apart from mentioning the Christian values of simplicity and gospel poverty in the context of the school ethos, *RDECS* also encourages pupils to take care of their schools as they would take care of the world and thereby grow in 'ecological awareness' (29). Catholic schools should educate people to work for the common good, to become more aware of international issues and to listen to the Church's regular appeals for 'peace, justice, freedom, progress...' (45). At a very practical level, *RDECS* asks that pupils should be taught at least some of the Church's social documents (90).[19] The proposed Leaving Certificate Section F, 3, is called 'The Religious Imperative to Act for Justice and Peace in relation to The Environment'. It goes even further than *RDECS*. In part 3g it presents 'the social teaching of the World Council of Churches and the Catholic Church – the teaching in action'. Clearly this proposed new syllabus is supportive of Catholic education at its best, in search of justice in an ecumenical spirit.

The school ethos

Another important theme is that of the school ethos or climate. As used in *RDECS*, this term refers to 'the sum total of the different components at work in the school which interact with one another in such a way as to create favourable conditions for a formation process' (24). This is a very positive definition of ethos. It describes an *ideal* to be aspired to and gradually realised. School ethos, however, can never be unaffected by the quality of the surrounding cultural climate. A major challenge before Catholic schools in Ireland today is to recognise the changing ethos of Irish life. This point has been made very forcefully by a young Religion teacher, who writes that, 'These are the nineties. And the new Ireland is here to stay. And Lent doesn't matter. Religion doesn't matter. For some at least. And the numbers are growing'.[20]

Ethos can be described as 'the way things are' in a school, as the sum of all the hidden assumptions and values and biases and prejudices that bring both life and death to all those in school. Ethos, in this broader sense, is not always recognised for what it is or for the power it wields. It is something implicit in everything that happens in school; it comes across to all in school as 'the familiar foot-steps of their minds'.[21] Sometimes the term 'hidden curriculum' is used to refer to school ethos. The assumption here is that over and above the obvious taught curriculum, as laid down in the syllabuses, there is another latent curriculum whose influence is substantial. To be aware of its influence is crucial for the provision of good education in school; but to call it 'hidden' seems to me to be a mistake. To anyone who takes time to reflect, not only is it not 'hidden', but in many ways it is the most visible, tangible and sensible reality in every school. It might more accurately be called the 'implicit curriculum', in contrast with the explicitly stated and taught curriculum, which of course is never the only or even the most powerful educational influence in the school.

In its analysis of educational ethos, *RDECS* stresses the importance of the very physical environment of the school. A school should be an extension of all that home provides by way of 'a pleasant and happy family atmosphere' (27). Though the prime responsibility for creating and maintaining this climate rests with the community of teachers, *RDECS* has a very inclusive notion of the overall school community, consisting of teachers, directors, administrative and auxiliary staff, parents and pupils (32). The Catholic school keeps open all channels of communication between all participants, and prides itself on their readiness to work collaboratively (39).[22] It aspires to becoming an open community, where the school is open to parents, to the local Church community and to civil society (42-46). To be Catholic is to be inclusive rather than exclusive, and therefore 'the Catholic school of the future ought to be distinctive in its critical openness to the modern and post-modern world'.[23]

An open Catholic school community, with complex networks of horizontal relationships, would also be characterised by ongoing vertical interaction, through prayer. Such prayer 'is the fullest and most complete expression' of the religious dimension of the Catholic school' (111). In this context, one is pleased to note the Junior Certificate Section E (*The Celebration of Faith*), as well as the proposed Leaving Certificate Section G on *Worship, Prayer and Ritual*.

Catechesis and religious instruction
The preparation of properly trained Religion teachers for Catholic schools ought to be a major concern of the Church (97). According to *RDECS*, the Religion teacher is the key to achieving the educational goals of the school (96). While recognising the religious dimension of

the culture in which young people live before they come to school
(7-23); while emphasising the religious value of a good school ethos
(24-46) and the religious dimension of the whole school curriculum
(47-61), *RDECS* still insists that the work of the Religion teacher is a
central part of the mission of the Catholic school. The ideal of
'interdisciplinary co-operation' (64) between all teachers in a Catholic
school is proposed, so that religious questions arising throughout the
curriculum can be addressed in an enriching manner. Christian faith
has a clear vision of what it means to be a human person, and this can
have many educational implications, for example, for the teaching of
science, poetry and physical education.[24]

But the role of the Religion teacher goes beyond such
interdisciplinary co-operation. The Religion teacher is primarily
concerned with 'the systematic presentation of religion' (65). As
models for such systematic teaching, *RDECS* develops two possible
outlines for teaching religion, one doctrinal, and the other with a
moral thrust (73-94). This latter outline of Christian ethics (especially
82-87) is well complemented by material in the new syllabuses,
especially Junior Certificate Section F (*The Moral Challenge*) and the
proposed Leaving Certificate Section D, part 1 on 'Thinking about
Morality', and part 2 on 'Morality and Religion'.

Within the work of the whole school, whose catechetical life is
rooted in a Christian ethos and whose catechetical activities take place
throughout the whole curriculum, the specific task of the Religion
teacher is to give religious instruction. Unlike catechesis, which
assumes that the hearer is freely listening to the Christian message as a
saving word, that this process takes place over a whole lifetime, and
that its aim is maturity of faith (68-69), religious instruction has a
narrower focus, a shorter timescale and a more modest aim. Religious
instruction is offered to a class of pupils, some of whom may not
believe or may not really want to be present. Faith may be there, but
it cannot be assumed in each case. The timescale of class work is very
limited; it takes place only two hours a week for about ten years. The
direct aim of religious instruction is not maturity of faith but
knowledge of faith.

Of course, it is possible that well-taught Religion classes will
provide such religious knowledge and understanding as will enable

young people to mature in whatever faith they may have. In this sense, 'religious instruction and catechesis are at the same time distinct and complementary' (70).[25] James Michael Lee argues forcefully for recognising the distinctiveness of catechesis and religious instruction. He suggests 'that learners should be taught religion in the church in such a manner that gradually, as pedagogically appropriate, they be given less and less catechesis and more and more religious instruction'.[25] The new syllabuses, in each of their sections, offer a statement of Aims and Objectives. Under Objectives, the proposed Leaving Certificate syllabus lists Knowledge, Understanding, Skills and Attitudes. It is *these* educational objectives that are the main thrust of both new Religious Education syllabuses, just as they are the main thrust of the religious instruction offered in the classrooms of the ideal Catholic school.

Conclusion

To capture the vision of *RDECS* regarding the teaching of Religion in Catholic schools, here is one of its strongest statements: 'religious instruction ... should have a place in the weekly order alongside the other classes ... it should have its own syllabus ... it should seek appropriate interdisciplinary links with other course material... Like other course work, it should promote culture, and it should make use of the best educational methods available... In some countries the results of examinations in religious knowledge are included within the overall measure of student progress. Finally, religious instruction in the school needs to be co-ordinated with the catechesis offered in parishes, in the family, and in youth associations' (70). From these aspirations, one can easily deduce that the ideal of Religious Instruction being proposed here for Catholic schools throughout the world is based on very sound educational theory, and is therefore quite consonant with the pattern of religious education outlined in the new Religious Education syllabuses.

Notes

1. See Second Vatican Council, *GE* (1965); and Sacred Congregation for Catholic Education, *CS* (1977), and *LCS* (1982). The most recent publication, *The Catholic School on the Threshold of the Third Millennium* (1998), is a brief statement of themes more fully developed in *RDECS*.

2. See D. Lane, 'Catholic Education and the School: Some Theological Reflections', in Conference of Major Religious Superiors, *The Catholic School in Contemporary Society*, pp. 81-100. For a masterly account of four different styles of school evaluation, see J. McDonagh, 'Catholic Education and Evaluation', *CSCS*, pp. 47-80. See also A. Donaldson and D. Breen, 'Catholic Education: Vocation or Profession?' in St Mary's CBGS, *EAE*, no. 3, Summer 1997, p. 8.

3. Sacred Congregation for Catholic Education, *RDECS*, par. 22, footnote 12. Subsequent references to the *RDECS* are given within the text, as follows: (22) refers to *RDECS*, par. 22.

4. M. P. Gallagher, in Hogan and Williams (eds.), *FRIE*, p. 25.

5. M. P. Gallagher, 'Post-Modernity: Friend or Foe?' in E. Cassidy (ed.), *FCIC*, p. 76.

6. M. P. Gallagher, *Clashing Symbols*, p. 123.

7. See N. Postman, *TACA*, p. 29.

8. Ibid. The main purpose of school teaching is thus to 'free the young from the tyranny of the present' (p. 40) and to offer 'an alternative to what the culture is doing' (p. 41).

9. See N. Brennan, 'Christian Education, Contestation and the Catholic School', in CMRS, *CSCS*, p. 15.

10. See P. Reilly, 'We must defend our schools', in *The Tablet* (28 November 1998), p. 1576.

11. See J. Arthur, *The Ebbing Tide*, p. 231.

12. P. Fogarty, *Why don't they believe in us?*, p. 107.

13. See M. Bradshaw, 'The Christian and Geographical Explanation', in L. Francis and A. Thatcher, *CPFE*, pp. 376-382.

14. A. Murphy, 'Music, Meaning and Mystery: Towards a Theophany of Music', in Lane (ed.), *RCD*, offers a very moving analysis of two pieces of modern music in terms of the mystery of death and afterlife (pp. 98-101).

15. E. Cassidy, 'Pathways to God: Beauty, the Road Less Travelled', in
    A. M. Murphy and E. Cassidy (eds.), *Neglected Wells*, p. 25. See
    also J. Devitt, 'Witnesses and Prophets: Some Soundings in
    Recent Irish Writing', which says that 'the richer and more
    abundant life we crave is prefigured in works of art' (*NW*, p. 136).
16. For good examples of such a debate see U. Agnew, 'The Poet and
    the Word: Spirituality in the Work of Patrick Kavanagh', and M.
    Kelleher, 'The Spiritual Strain in Contemporary Women's
    Writings' in *NW*. For an exploration of the paradox of
    imagination and constraint within education, through an analysis
    of poetry within the bureaucratic structures of school, see D.
    Campfield, 'Outrageous Inscapes (Poetry, Selfhood and
    Delinquency)' in St Mary's CBGS, *EAE,* no. 3 (Summer 1997).
17. See J. Devitt, 'Where Hope and History Rhyme: The Poetry of
    Seamus Heaney', in D. A. Lane (ed.) *RCD*, p. 119.
18. K. Williams, in Hogan and Williams (eds.), *FRIE,* p. 14.
19.   See *RDECS*, footnote 95. I have developed this idea in
    Chapter 9.
20. A. Looney, 'Disappearing Echoes, New Voices and the Sounds of
    Silence', in S. Mac Réamoinn (ed.), *CNI*, p. 28.
21. See J. Dunne, 'The Catholic School and Civil Society: Exploring
    the Tensions', in CMRS, *CSCS*, p. 27.
22. The ideal of a collaborative staff is discussed by M. Crawford and
    G. Rossiter in 'Developing Staff Spirituality: Key Component of
    the Identity of Catholic Schools', *CSS,* 66. no. 1 (May 1993), pp.
    27-32.
23. D. A. Lane, 'The Expanding Horizons of Catholic Education', in
    Hogan and Williams (eds.), *FRIE,* p. 137.
24. See A. Thatcher, 'Learning to become persons: a theological
    approach to educational aims', in L. Francis and A. Thatcher
    (eds.), *CPFE* .
25. See G. Rossiter, 'The need for "a creative divorce" between
    catechesis and religious education in Catholic schools', Religious
    Education Association, *Religious Education,* 77 (1982), pp. 21-40.
26. See J. M. Lee, 'Catechesis Sometimes, Religious Instruction
    Always', in M. Mayr (ed.), *DCRWRE*, p. 66.

BIBLIOGRAPHY

WITH ACRONYMS FOR REGULARLY OCCURRING TITLES

Anouilh, J. *Antigone* (London: Eyre Methuen, 1973).

Aotearoa/New Zealand Catholic Bishops' Conference. *Understanding Faith* series (Auckland: National Centre for Religious Studies, 1991). (*UF*)

Arias, J. *Prayer Without Frills* (Cork: Mercier, 1975).

Arthur, J. *The Ebbing Tide* (Leominster: Gracewing, 1995).

Astley, J. *The Philosophy of Christian Religious Education* (Birmingham, Alabama: REP, 1994). (*PCRE*)

Australian Province Leaders of the Christian Brothers. *Catholic School Studies* (Parkville, Australia). (*CSS*)

Bailey, K.E. *Poet and Peasant* and *Through Peasant Eyes: A Literary-Cultural Approach to the Parables of Luke* (Combined Edition), (Grand Rapids, Michigan: William B. Eerdmans, 1990).

Balasuriya, T., *Eucharist and Human Liberation* (London: SCM Press, 1979).

Benedictine monks. *The Book of Saints*, A Dictionary of Servants of God Canonised by the Catholic Church (London: Cassell, 1994).

Boran, G. The Pastoral Challenges of a New Age (Dublin: Veritas, 1999).

Bosch, D. J. *Transforming Mission* (New York: Orbis, 1994).

Boyers, J. *Religious Meaning-Making* (Unpublished, Limited Print, Revised and Enlarged, 1994).

———— *Religion Class Talk: An Examination of the Language and Logic of Religious Education* (Unpublished, Limited Print, Revised and Enlarged, 1994).

Brown, R. *The Churches the Apostles Left Behind* (London: Geoffrey Chapman, 1984).

Brueggemann, W. *The Prophetic Imagination* (Philadelphia: Fortress Press, fifth printing, 1983).

———— *The Bible and Postmodern Imagination* (London: SCM Press, 1993).

————— *The Bible Makes Sense* (Revised edition), (Winona, Minne: St Mary's Press, 1997).

Bryk, A. S. Lee, V. E. and Holland, P. B., *Catholic Schools and the Common Good* (Harvard: Harvard University Press, 1993).

Callaghan, J. and Cockett, M. *Are Our Schools Christian?* (Great Wakering: Mayhew McCrimmon, 1975).

Caprio, B. *Experiments in Prayer* (Notre Dame, Indiana: Ave Maria Press, 1973).

Cardinal, M. *The Words to Say It* (Cambridge, Mass.: Van Victor and Goodheart, 1984).

Cassidy, E. (ed.) *Faith and Culture in the Irish Context* (Dublin: Veritas, 1996). *(FCIC)*

Catechetical Association of Ireland. *The Irish Catechist* (Dublin). (IrCat)

————— Newsletter (Dublin).

Catholic Bishops' Conference of England and Wales. *Religious Education: Curriculum Directory for Catholic Schools* (London: Catholic Education Service, 1996).

————— *Statement on Religious Education in Catholic Schools* (London: Catholic Media Office, 2000).

Chatwin, B. *The Songlines* (London: Picador, 1988).

Christian Education Movement. *British Journal of Religious Education* (Derby). *(BJRE)*

Clark, T. C. (compiler) *1000 Quotable Poems* (New York: Bonanza Books, 1985).

Clement of Alexandria, *Paidagogos (Christ the Educator),* (Washington D.C.: Catholic University of America Press, 1954).

Coggan, D. *The Prayers of the New Testament* (London: Hodder and Stoughton, 1967).

Coleman, J. S. and Hoffer, T. *Public and Private High Schools: The Impact of Communities* (New York: Basic Books, 1987).

Conference of Major Religious Superiors. *The Catholic School in Contemporary Society* (Dublin: 1991). *(CSCS)*

Conroy, J. C. (ed.) *Catholic Education: Inside-Out, Outside-In* (Dublin: Veritas, 1999).

Convey, M. A. *Keeping the Faith in a Changing Society* (Dublin: Columba Press, 1994).

Cooling, T. *Concept Cracking: Exploring Christian Beliefs in School* (Stapleford: Association of Christian Teachers, 1994).

Corbishley, T. *The Prayer of Jesus* (London: Mowbrays, 1976).

Crawford, M. and Rossiter, G. *Teaching Religion in the Secondary School* (Sydney: Christian Brothers, 1985). *(TRSS)*

——— *Missionaries to a Teenage Culture* (Sydney: Christian Brothers, 1988). *(MTC)*

Crichton, J. D. *The Once and Future Liturgy* (Dublin: Veritas, 1977).

De Benedittis, S.M. *Teaching Faith and Morals* (Minneapolis: Winston Press, 1981).

Del Prete, T. *Thomas Merton and the Education of the Whole Person* (Birmingham, Alabama: REP, 1990).

Devitt, P. M. *How Adult is Adult Religious Education?: Gabriel Moran's Contribution to the Field of Adult Religious Education* (Dublin: Veritas, 1991).

——— *That You May Believe: A Brief History of Religious Education* (Dublin: Dominican Publications, 1992). *(TYMB)*

——— *Immortal Diamond: Facets of Mature Faith* (Dublin: Veritas, 1997). *(ID)*

Devitt, P. M. (ed.) *A Companion to the Catechism* (Dublin: Veritas, 1995). *(CC)*

Doherty, M. M. *Dynamic Approaches to Teaching High School Religion* (New York: Alba House, 1969).

Dominican Publications. *Doctrine and Life* (Dublin), *(DL)*

Dorr, D. *Option for the Poor* (Dublin: Gill and Macmillan, 1983).

——— *Spirituality and Justice* (Dublin: Gill and Macmillan, 1984).

——— *Integral Spirituality* (Dublin: Gill and Macmillan, 1990).

Drumm, M. *Passage to Pasch: Revisiting the Catholic Sacraments* (Dublin: Columba Press, 1998).

Drumm, M. and Gunning, T. *A Sacramental People, Vols. 1, 2* (Dublin: Columba Press, 1999, 2000).

Duffy, E. *Saints and Sinners: A History of the Popes* (Yale University Press, 1997).

Durka, G. and Smith, J. *Emerging Issues in Religious Education* (New York: Paulist Press, 1976).

Dykstra, C. *Vision and Character: A Christian Educator's Alternative to Kohlberg* (New York: Paulist Press, 1981).

Dykstra, C. and Parks, S. (eds.) *Faith Development and Fowler* (Birmingham, Alabama: REP, 1986).

Fahy, P. S. *Faith in Catholic Classrooms* (Homebush, NSW: St. Paul Publication, 1992). *(FCC)*

Feheney, J. M. (ed.). *Beyond the Race for Points: Aspects of Pastoral Care in a Catholic School Today* (Dublin: Veritas, 1999).

Feheney, J. M. *From Ideal to Action: The Inner Nature of a Catholic School Today* (Dublin: Veritas, 1998).

Felderhof, M. C. (ed.), *Religious Education in a Pluralist Society* (London: Hodder and Stoughton, 1985).

Flanagan, B. *The Spirit of the City: Voices from Dublin's Liberties* (Dublin: Veritas, 1999).

Finley, J. and Pennock, M. *Your Faith and You* (Notre Dame, Indiana: Ave Maria Press, 1978).

Fogarty, P. *Why Don't They Believe In Us? Handing on the Faith in a Changing Society* (Dublin: Columba Press, 1993).

Fowler, J. W. *Stages of Faith: The Psychology of Human Development and the Quest for Meaning* (San Francisco: Harper and Row, 1981).

Francis, L. and Thatcher, A. (eds.) *Christian Perspectives for Education* (Leominster: Fowler Wright Books, 1990). *(CPFE)*

——— *Studies in Religion and Education* (London: Falmer Press, 1984).

Furrow Trust, *The Furrow* (Naas, Co. Kildare).

Gaffney, J. *Focus on Doctrine* (New York: Paulist Press, 1973).

Gallagher, M. P. *Clashing Symbols: An Introduction to Faith and Culture* (London: Darton, Longman and Todd, 1997).

Gelineau, J. *The Liturgy Today and Tomorrow* (London: Darton, Longman and Todd, 1978).

Gillespie, V. B. *The Experience of Faith* (Birmingham, Alabama: REP, 1988).

Girzone, J. F. *Joshua: A Parable for Today* (New York: Macmillan, 1987).

Glazier, M. and Hellwig, M. K. (eds.) *The Modern Catholic Encyclopedia*, (Dublin: Gill and Macmillan, 1994).

Grassi, J. A. *Jesus as Teacher* (Winona, Minnesota: St Mary's College Press, 1978).

Greeley, A. *The Great Mysteries* (Dublin: Gill and Macmillan, 1977).

Grey, M., Heaton, A. and Sullivan, D. (eds.) *The Candles Are Still Burning* (London: Geoffrey Chapman, 1995).

Griffith, B. *The Marriage of East and West* (London: Collins, 1982).

Grimmitt, M. *Religious Education and Human Development* (Great Wakering: McCrimmons, 1987).

Groome, T. *Christian Religious Education* (San Francisco: Harper and Row, 1980).

Groome, T. H. *Education for Life: A Spiritual Vision for Every Teacher and Parent* (Allen, Texas: Thomas More, 1998). *(EFL)*

Hanly, M. *Ireland's Link with the Global Refugee Crisis* (Dublin: Refugee Trust, 1997).

Harrington, D. *What is Morality?* (Dublin: Columba Press, 1996).

Harris, M. *Teaching and Religious Imagination* (San Francisco: Harper and Row, 1987).

Harris, M. and Moran, G. *Reshaping Religious Education: Conversations on Contemporary Practice* (Louisville, Kentucky: Westminster John Knox Press, 1998).

Hill, B. R. *Key Dimensions of Religious Education* (Winona, Minnesota: St Mary's Press, 1988).

Hogan, P. *The Custody and Courtship of Experience: Western Education in Philosophical Perspective* (Dublin: Columba Press, 1995).

Hogan, P. and Williams, K. (eds.) *The Future of Religion in Irish Education* (Dublin: Veritas, 1997). *(FRIE)*

Hollings, M. and Gillick, E. *It's Me, O Lord* (London: Hodder and Stoughton, 1972).

Hulmes, E. *Commitment and Neutrality in Religious Education* (London: Geoffrey Chapman, 1979).

Hyland, J. (ed.) *Mary in the Church* (Dublin: Veritas, 1989). *(MIC)*

International Centre for Studies in Religious Education, *Lumen Vitae* (Brussels). *(LV)*

Irish Bishops, *Conscience* (Dublin: Veritas, 1998).

Irish Catholic Bishops' Conference. *Guidelines for the Faith Formation and Development of Catholic Students: Junior Certificate Religious Education Syllabus.* Compiled by Caroline Renehan, Director, National Catechetical Office (Dublin: Veritas, 1999).

John Paul II. *Catechesi tradendae* (Rome: 1979).

_____ *Catechism of the Catholic Church* (Rome: 1994). *(CCC)*

Johnston, E. *Friends of God and Prophets: A Feminist Theological Reading of the Communion of Saints* (London: SCM Press, 1998).

Jungmann, J. A. *The Good News Yesterday and Today* (New York: Sadlier, 1962).

Kelly, K. *From a Parish Base: Essays in Moral and Pastoral Theology* (London: DLT, 1999).

Küng, H. *Eternal Life?* (London: Collins, 1984). *(EL)*

Lane, D. A. (ed.) *Religious Education and the Future* (Dublin: Columba Press, 1986). *(REF)*

_____ *Religion, Education and the Constitution* (Dublin: Columba Press, 1992).

_____ *Religion and Culture in Dialogue: A Challenge for the Next Millennium* (Dublin: Columba Press, 1993). *(RCD)*

Larkin, T. and McAndrew, P. *The GATEWAY series: A Mission, Justice and Development Manual for Religious Educators* (Navan, Co. Meath: Columban Fathers and Sister).

Lee, J. M. *The Flow of Religious Instruction* (Dayton, Ohio:Pflaum/ Standard, 1973).

Lewis, C. S. *Mere Christianity* (London: Collins, 1952).

McCarthy, L. S. *Creating Space for R.E. The Ballygall Project: Theory and Practice* (Dublin: Columba Press, 1986).

McDonagh, S. *The Greening of the Church* (London: Geoffrey Chapman, 1990).

McFague, S. *Metaphorical Theology* (London, SCM Press, 1982).

McFarland, H. S. N. *Intelligent Teaching* (London: Routledge and Kegan Paul, 1973).

Mac Réamoinn, S. (ed.), *The Church in a New Ireland* (Dublin: Columba Press, 1996). *(CNI)*

Macquarrie, J. *Mary for all Christians* (London: Collins, 1990).

Maher, M. (ed.) *Irish Spirituality* (Dublin: Veritas, 1981).

Marino, J. S. (ed.) *Biblical Themes in Religious Education* (Birmingham, Alabama: REP, 1983). *(BTRE)*

Marmion, J. P. *Catholic Traditions in Education* (Macclesfield: St Edward's Press, 1986).

Marthaler, B. *Catechetics in Context* (Huntington, Indiana: Our Sunday Visitor, 1973).

———— *The Creed* (Mystic, Conn.: Twenty-Third Publications, 1987).

Mayhew McCrimmon, *The Sower* (Great Wakering, Essex).

Mayr, M. (ed.) *Does the Church Really Want Religious Education?* (Birmingham, Alabama: REP, 1988). *(DCRWRE)*

Miller, R.C. (ed.), *Theologies of Religious Education* (Birmingham, Alabama: REP, 1995). *(TRE)*

Monahan, L. and Renehan, C. *The Chaplain: A Faith Presence in the School Community* (Dublin: Columba, 1998).

Moran, G. *God Still Speaks* (London, Search Press, 1967). *(GSS)*

———— *Design for Religion* (London: Search Press, 1970).

———— *Religious Education Development* (Minneapolis: Winston Press, 1983).

———— *No Ladder to the Sky: Education and Morality* (San Francisco: Harper and Row, 1987).

———— *Religious Education as a Second Language* (Birmingham, Alabama: REP, 1989). *(REASL)*

———— *Showing How: The Act of Teaching* (Valley Forge, Pennsylvania: Trinity Press International, 1997).

Morwood, M. *Tomorrow's Catholic: Understanding God and Jesus in a New Millennium* (Mystic, Connecticut: Twenty-Third Publications, 1997).

Murphy, C. C. *An Introduction to Christian Feminism* (Dublin: Dominican Publications, 1994).

Murphy, A. M. and Cassidy, E. (eds.) *Neglected Wells: Spirituality and the Arts* (Dublin: Veritas, 1997). *(NW)*

Murray, D. *Jesus is Lord* (Dublin: Veritas, 1973). *(JL)*

———— *The Future of the Faith* (Dublin: Veritas, 1985).

———— *Secularism and the New Europe* (Dublin: Veritas, 1990).

———— *A Special Concern. The Philosophy of Education: A Christian Perspective* (Dublin: Veritas, 1991).

National Council for Curriculum and Assessment. *Redraft Syllabuses for Religious Education* (Dublin: May 1997).

Neary, D. *Calm Beneath the Storm* (Dublin: Veritas, 1983).

———— *Prayer Services for Young People* (Dublin: Columba Press, 1986).

———— *Praying in Advent* (Dublin: Columba Press, 1987).

———— *Come and Pray* (Dublin: Columba Press, 1988).

———— *Praying in Lent* (Dublin: Columba Press, 1989).

———— *Praying at Easter* (Dublin: Columba Press, 1991).

———— *Pilgrim in Lent* (Dublin: Columba Press, 1992).

———— *Pilgrim in Advent* (Dublin: Columba Press, 1994).

———— *Lighting the Shadows* (Dublin: Veritas, 1995).

Nichols, K. *Cornerstone* (Slough: St Paul Publications, 1978).

———— *Orientations* (Middlegreen, Slough: St Paul's, 1979).

———— *Refracting the Light: Learning the Languages of Faith* (Dublin: Veritas, 1997).

O'Brien, J. *Seeds of a New Church* (Dublin: Columba Press, 1994).

O'Brien, N. *Revolution from the Heart* (Dublin: Veritas, 1987).

O'Connor, P. *Emerging Voices: Women in Contemporary Irish Society* (Dublin: IPA, 1998).

O'Donohue, J. *Anam Chara* (London: Bantam Press, 1997).

O'Dwyer, P. *Mary: A History of Irish Devotion* (Dublin: Four Courts Press, 1988).

O'Hare, P. (ed.) *Foundations of Religious Education* (New York: Paulist Press, 1978).

———— *Education for Peace and Justice* (San Francisco: Harper&Row, 1983). *(EPJ)*

O'Leary, D. (ed.) *Religious Education and Young Adults* (Slough: St Paul's, 1983). *(REYA)*

Oser, F. and Gmünder, P. *Religious Judgement: A Developmental Approach* (Birmingham, Alabama: Religious Education Press, 1991).

Osiek, C. *Beyond Anger: On Being a Feminist in the Church* (Dublin: Gill and Macmillan, 1986).

Our Sunday Visitor. *PACE* 11 (Huntington, Indiana: 1982).

Postman, N. *Teaching as a Conserving Activity* (New York: Dell Publishing, 1979). *(TACA)*

Purnell, A. P. *Our Faith Story* (London: Collins, 1985).

Quoist, M. *Prayers of Life* (Dublin: Gill, 1963).

Rahner, K. *Theological Investigations* (London: Darton, Longman and Todd, 1965-92).

Reichert, R. *A Learning Process for Religious Education* (Dayton: Pflaum Publishing, 1975).

Religious Education Association. *Religious Education* (Fair Haven, CT).

Sacred Congregation for Catholic Education, *The Catholic School* (Rome: 1977). *(CS)*

———— *Lay Catholics in Schools: Witnesses to Faith* (Rome: 1982). *(LCS)*

———— *The Religious Dimension of Education in a Catholic School* (Rome: 1988). *(RDECS)*

Sacred Congregation of the Clergy, *Directorium Catechisticum Generale* (Rome: 1971). In translation, *General Catechetical Directory (GCD)*

———— *General Directory for Catechesis* (Rome: 1997). *(GDC)*

Sawicki, M. *The Gospel in History* (New York: Paulist Press, 1988).

Schipani, D.S. *Religious Education encounters Liberation Theology* (Birmingham, Alabama: REP, 1988).

Schnackenburg, R. *Jesus in the Gospels: A Biblical Christology* (Louisville, Kentucky: Westminster John Knox Press, 1995).

Second Vatican Council, *Gravissimum educationis* (Rome: 1965). *(GE)*

Shannon, W. H. *Seeking the Face of God* (New York: Collins, 1988).

Smith, C. *The Way of Paradox: Spiritual Life as taught by Meister Eckhart* (London: Darton, Longman and Todd, 1987).

St Mary's CBGS, *Ethos and Education* (Belfast). *(EAE)*

Sullivan, J. *Catholic Schools in Contention: Competing Metaphors and Leadership Implications* (Dublin: Veritas, 2000).

The Tablet Publishing Company, *The Tablet* (London).

Thompson, N. (ed.) *Religious Education and Theology* (Birmingham, Alabama, REP, 1982).

Thurston, A. *Because of her Testimony: The Word in Female Experience* (Dublin: Gill and Macmillan, 1993).

Tilley, T. W. *Story Theology* (Wilmington, Delaware: Michael Glazier, 1985).

Treston, K. *Paths and Stories: Spirituality for Teachers and Catechists* (Dublin: Veritas, 1991).

Tugwell, S. *Prayer* (Dublin: Veritas, 1974).

United States Catholic Conference, Department of Education, *The Living Light* (Washington DC). *(LL)*

Vanier, J. *Community and Growth* (London: DLT, 1979).

Warner, M. *Alone of All her Sex* (London: Picador, 1976).

Watson, B. *The Effective Teaching of RE* (London: Longman, 1993). *(ETRE)*

Weafer, J. A. and Hanley, A. *Whither Religious Education?* (Dublin: Columba Press, 1991).

Weil, S. *Gateway to God* (Glasgow: Collins, 1974).

Zappone, K. *The Hope for Wholeness: A Spirituality for Feminists* (Mystic, Conn.: Twenty-Third Publications, 1991).

INDEX